RADICAL CAREER CHANGE

RADICAL CAREER CHANGE

LIFE BEYOND WORK

David L. Krantz

THE FREE PRESS
A Division of Macmillan Publishing Co., Inc.
NEW YORK

Collier Macmillan Publishers
LONDON

Copyright © 1978 by The Free Press

A Division of Macmillan Publishing Co., Inc.

The Free Press
A Division of Macmillan Publishing Co., Inc.
866 Third Avenue, New York, N.Y. 10022

Collier Macmillan Canada, Ltd.

Library of Congress Catalog Card Number: 78-50720

Printed in the United States of America

printing number
1 2 3 4 5 6 7 8 9 10

Library of Congress Cataloging in Publication Data

Krantz, David L
    Radical career change.

    1. Occupational mobility—United States—Psychological aspects. 2. Professions—United States. 3. Adulthood. I. Title.
HD8038.U5K7   155.2'5   78–50720
ISBN 0–02–916760–4

To
Santa Fe, New Mexico,
and
Claire Krantz,
who helped me understand myself
in that world

CONTENTS

FOREWORD

David Krantz's *Radical Career Change* is in some ways a lineal descendant of that great American book *The Education of Henry Adams* (1907), a critical view of the modern world that defies precise labeling as autobiography, social history, or philosophy but that is, I think, undeniably a great book. Adams was one of the first American writers (certainly one of the best) to confront the dilemmas of personal growth in our society. What shapes a person? What are the formal and informal sources of education? How, if ever, does the child, adolescent, and young adult emerge from the fog of youth with purpose and direction? Without the God of religion, how does one judge where he has been, is, and wants to be? And how can we answer these questions, Adams asks, living as we do in a world where we seem to be such frequent victims of the laws of chance as well as of social forces before which we are impotent?

As he so frequently reminds the reader, Adams was born in the mid-nineteenth century into an eighteenth-century family unequipped to deal with the twentieth-century world (which began to emerge long before 1901). He was quintessentially the inner-directed man whose strength exacerbated the conflicts between him and his society, between stasis and change, and between his and society's definition of the good life. He was a quester, a soaker-up of experience, a participant and a spectator at the same time. He was as hard on himself as he was on the world around him. He knew where he came from and who he was. He was an Adams. But that knowledge, in the modern world, was insufficient to answer the questions of how he wanted to live and what he wanted to be.

In confronting these questions, Adams did not, as did so

many writers after him, trivialize them by purely psychological explanation. He was too much an Adams, a historian, a medievalist, to see himself other than in a ceaseless flow of social history, a recipient of gifts from the past unsuited to a changing society. He mocked and belittled the emerging modern world, not only because it was such a contrast to the values and traditions of the Adams family in Quincy (*not* Boston, he emphasizes) but because it was a world that confused change with progress, and movement with purpose.

The reader who has first read *The Education of Henry Adams* will better appreciate the significance of Krantz's book. Consider the title and substance of Krantz's last chapter, "Collapsing Frames," a vivid phrase describing a kind of isomorphism between an individual's private, anxious quest for meaning and purpose, on the one hand, and, on the other hand, a world "out there" seeking a substitute for the transcendence and social cohesion religion used to promise and give, a world disappointed in its hope that science and technology would solve its problems. Henry Adams would nod and say, "So what is new?" A major theme of Adams's book is collapsing frames. However, the people Krantz writes about are trying to discover who they are, trying to plumb that core of "real" self, changing from one basis of living to another, trying to go back to "first principles." Henry Adams knew who he was and where he came from, and that was as much a source of solace and pride as it was of aloofness and self-derogation. Although he saw his social frames collapsing, his sense of self did not alter.

But Adams's book was written more than three-quarters of a century ago. Could it be written today? Would the people Krantz writes about see any degree of kinship with Adams? Would they envy, be puzzled by, or laugh at Adams's sense of family and continuity? Would they comprehend his sense of obligation to his society, his inability or refusal to retreat into an indulgence of self? From Krantz's poignant descriptions and incisive discussion I have to conclude that his "subjects" would be much more aware of differences than of similarities. The world has indeed changed, and in ways that Adams feared, and if he had doubts that he would be understood in his own time, he probably had none about the distant future.

No one who has read *The Education of Henry Adams* would say that the title reflects the contents, scope, and depth of the book. Similarly, no one who reads Krantz's book will say that "radical career change" or Santa Fe as a special place is what the book is about. His is a book about us (and him) and our society, about the sources of our "education," and how we have been hoist by our own petard. We have been taught that we may expect great things in life, that all problems are solvable, that we are and can be many things in life, that we should do our "own thing," that education for professionalism is a must if one wants to lead an endlessly fascinating and comfortable existence. Call them what you will, these are messages to *individuals* about *individual* goals and living. That the individual psyche is formed in an ever-changing social context, in a continuous series of presents that contain remnants of diverse pasts (the characteristics of social context are never born yesterday, or last year, or even a decade ago), has not been part of the message. Quite the contrary, part of the message—and since World War II it has been an important part—is that young people should escape from a past to which their elders have been victim and from which a crazy world has emerged.

That such a message would produce more rudderless lives Henry Adams knew and David Krantz describes so well. A colleague of mine said about a student, "He went to Europe to find himself, except he wasn't there." I do not quote my colleague to mock the student. Far from it, because the statement illuminates (albeit unwittingly) the emphasis people put on self-discovery and their deemphasis of the relationship between what they think they have discovered and the external structure of that world "out there." That world, of course, is no less structured, no less complicated, no less full of tensions and conflicts, no less conscious and unconscious of its nature and the intended and unintended consequences of its purposes than the individual psyche. What the author of this book has done is to let people describe what happened to them when their eyes opened to the obvious and they were forced to play back their pasts to see where they went wrong. And what struck me with great force as I read what these people were thinking and experiencing is their continued emphasis on self.

There is an artistry in the structure of this book. Krantz gets out of the way of his subjects and only minimally interposes himself between them and the reader. Inevitably, therefore, the reader has to do a lot of thinking for himself, that is, to take what these people are saying and make sense of it. Many, perhaps most, readers will feel some degree of kinship with the interviewees, even though they are reading the book in New York, Atlanta, Chicago, Indianapolis, New Haven, or wherever. More than a few may be so taken with Krantz's descriptions of Santa Fe's ambience, landscape, and colors (literally) that they will go there. And, of course, some readers, far from feeling any kinship, will pass a negative judgment on "those" people, who, they hope, are few in number and who, they are glad to conclude, deserve each other.

Although reactions to the interviews will vary, I believe the response will be unanimous when readers come to the last chapter, where David Krantz calls for the curtain, stands in front of it, and tells the audience the sense he makes of it all. It is wonderful sense. Yes, Henry Adams would indeed say, "So what is new?" Yes, others before and after Adams saw it clear and whole, and in broad outline predicted the course of the future. But that in no way detracts from Krantz's achievement. His aim is not to say something new, but rather to paint old truths in new ways so that when we are through with the book we know we needed to be reminded of what he has told us, and we are grateful.

When I finished reading this book, I was relieved that the

author resisted coming up with solutions. In the past decade there has been an explosion of books, journal articles, and mass media reports on the midcareer crisis, suggesting that, like drug abuse, alcoholism, swinging, and loneliness, it is on the rise and shouldn't we do something about it? Maybe pass or change laws, change the curriculum in our public schools, offer new courses in our colleges, or make this or that therapy more available to more people. No one wants to change the world more than I do—or David Krantz does. But when I look at proffered solutions I have to conclude that tunnel vision is a widespread malady. Henry Adams knew that too. And, I am glad to say, so does David Krantz.

Seymour B. Sarason

ACKNOWLEDGMENTS

My sincere thanks go to the Center for Advanced Study in the Behavioral Sciences for providing the opportunity to write this book. I was given not only the needed external support for my work—funds (from the Andrew W. Mellon Foundation and the National Science Foundation: NSF-BNS 76-22943), space, and unfettered time —but also the possibility to interact with colleagues from other disciplines, particularly James Freeman, and with my skillful and supportive secretary, Joan Warmbrunn. Perhaps the greatest gift the center offered was an atmosphere that promoted and deepened scholarship.

RADICAL CAREER CHANGE

OF HUMAN INTEREST

What would life be like without having to work, with little constraint or responsibility? I often wondered about that question, dreaming of the many pleasures I could enjoy if that fantasy became real.

That dream accidentally came true during my sabbatical in 1972. Because of administrative and political tangles, my year's research had come to an abrupt halt after six months. I was suddenly living out my fantasy of no work, no responsibility, on a full salary. After a few weeks of glorying in my new-found freedom, I found myself struggling to impose a meaningful structure on what seemed like an endless flow of time. The task became increasingly difficult. With no framework of responsibility, either to work or to family, defining my activities, I was soon at loose ends, discontent with my obligation only to "enjoy myself." After four months of living my fantasy, I began to look forward eagerly to resuming my regular job. Somehow the world of work had now assumed a positive glow.

Shortly before returning to my job, I met a fellow psychologist, Seymour Sarason. Among the issues that concerned him was the great difficulty people experienced in their world of work. I found his views sensible and intellectually stimulating, and over the course of a month we explored a broad range of thoughts and feelings on the subject. One of our discussions in particular provided the basis for the research reported in this book.

We agreed that a lot of people felt trapped by their work. They got little fulfillment or satisfaction from it, just a paycheck. That didn't seem to be enough. Most people tried to find some other outlet for their energy—hobbies, vacations, anything to make that awful trip down to the office worth something. Were there any other alternatives? Why not say "To hell with it all"? Just not work. No, we decided; even if you could afford it, what would you do with your time? Well, what about changing careers or jobs? Maybe making a really radical change? There had been an item in the newspaper the day before, about a banker who had chucked it all to become a waiter. He worked part of the day and then skied the rest. Not a bad life, we agreed. We wondered whether it really worked. I decided to see if I could learn anything more about the story.

After this discussion, I reread the newspaper item. The story was brief, tucked away on a back page as a filler. I called the local paper for more information but was told only that the item had come from a wire service. Checking with the wire service, I found out little more. Such fillers were submitted by local correspondents. They were always short, provocative pieces—just human interest items, the man told me. Readers got a kick out of them, liked them almost more than the daily news pieces.

After I hung up, I began to wonder why these articles are called "human interest" items and why readers find them so fascinating. Part of their appeal seems to lie in what is novel, exotic, unexpected—like the punch line of a joke. Fillers interest us because they provide departures from the sameness of our everyday lives. We take pleasure in reading them as we do in walking through the freak show of a circus. Fascinated by the aberrations of human life, we yet remain confident that we are safely normal, that extraordinary things happen to others but are unlikely to happen to us.

As I reflected on this, I began to realize that my concern with the problems of work and the possibility of radical career change was no longer solely intellectual—that protective detachment was decreasing. I remembered my reaction some fifteen years earlier on reading a similar human interest item. Then I had been shocked and dismayed by a story of a college professor who had given up his career to become a construction worker. Just beginning my own teaching career, I could not comprehend why anyone would abandon such a prestigious position for so minor a life station as "construction worker." But now my reaction was simply acceptance. The option of radical change seemed plausible, even sensible. Why had my reaction changed so dramatically over this fifteen-year period?

Part of the explanation lies in the reading I had done during that time. From the research literature on work* and on adult development,† I had learned much.

One important set of considerations involved the changing world of the professional. Since World War II there has been an explosion of new fields and career possibilities, creating in turn a burgeoning group of professionals in our work force. Yet, for all these possibilities, professionals remain generally fixed in the societal prescription of "one life, one career." What happens to the one who gets bored or seeks to broaden his career options? Change is not easy. Now more than ever, new career options require specialization and training. Even if the would-be career changer should seek further education, he would likely find that the available training facilities are already oversubscribed. And this very insufficiency of training

* See Seymour B. Sarason, *Work, Aging, and Social Change* (New York: Free Press, 1977).

† See Erik Erikson's theoretical perspective in *Childhood and Society* (New York: Norton, 1950). Among the empirical studies, see Roger Gould, "The Phases of Adult Life: A Study in Development," *American Journal of Psychiatry* 129 (1972): 521–31; Daniel Levinson et al., "The Psychosocial Development of Men in Early Adulthood and the Mid-life Transition," in D. F. Ricks et al. (eds.), *Life History Research in Psychopathology* (Minneapolis: University of Minnesota Press, 1974); Bernice Neugarten, "A Developmental View of Adult Personality," in James E. Birren (ed.), *Relations of Development and Aging* (Springfield, Ill.: Thomas, 1965); George Valliant, *Adaptation to Life* (Boston: Little, Brown, 1977). For a less technical treatment of this literature, see Gail Sheehy, *Passages* (New York: Dutton, 1974).

opportunities may have been one basis for his present dissatisfaction. If he was initially unable to obtain the necessary
education for the career he most wanted, he would have had
to settle for his second or third option. Working a lifetime in
a less than acceptable career is bound to create dissatisfaction.

Another consequence of increasingly educating our work
force is a heightening of expectations. Higher education tends
to underline the belief that work should be meaningful, that
the individual should experience satisfaction and fulfillment
through his work. The expectations of highly educated professionals are, it seems, as often disappointed as those of less
well trained workers; there is a rising trend of career change
within and between professional fields. Unless the future
world of work changes to meet the expectations of the increasing number of professionals, or unless those expectations are
modified, radical career change may become the wave of the
future.

Interacting with these historical and demographic changes
is the experiential world of the individual. Although adults
have probably always experienced concerns about work and
the meaning of life, it has only been within recent years that
social scientists have studied the psychological world of the
adult. Before these investigations, the adult years had been
viewed as a relatively undifferentiated, unchanging period, a
stable interval between the dramatically changing stages of
youth and the problems of old age. Current research has
shown that the adult years are filled with constantly changing
experiences, a kaleidoscopic world reflecting such complex and
interrelated concerns as identity, work, and family. These
changes have become symbolized in the phenomenon of midlife crisis. It is a time of turmoil, of questioning life's meaning
and purpose. Its drama is heightened by its place between the
relative peace of the preceding period and the calm of the
resolution that often follows.

Taken together, these insights provided me with an intelligible framework for understanding radical career change.

Yet, my awareness of this research literature explains only part of my increased acceptance of radical career change as a plausible solution to the dilemmas of work and of living. There was also a personal part. In that fifteen-year period, I found myself sharing similar feelings and experiences with those professionals and midlife-crisis people described in articles and books. I, too, increasingly felt trapped by my work. I, too, wondered about meaning and purpose in living. I could even project myself into the place of that college professor turned construction worker.

But there remained a crucial, unanswered question: what stopped me and all other dissatisfied professionals from becoming human interest items? For me, I had to know, if I were even to consider making such a change, whether that college professor had found a reasonable solution to his problems by making his radical change. Some guarantee of success, even if it were someone else's, would make my own difficult decision easier.

Being a social scientist, I decided to objectify my concerns by studying them "out there." Unfortunately, the existing research literature provided no direct answers to my specific research questions. I wanted to know what conditions led people to make a radical shift. What issues were they trying to resolve? To what extent did a radical shift in career require a change in geographical setting? What contributed to making their new lives better (or, perhaps, worse) than their former ones? Given the paucity of available information, it became clear that answers to the questions could be found only in the stories of people who had made a radical change.

My first task was to locate such people. From reading newspapers and talking with my friends, it seemed that Santa Fe, New Mexico, would be a likely place to find them. For my friends and me the name of Santa Fe evoked vague memories of some person who had changed his career and settled out there. Santa Fe, and nearby Taos, also projected an ill-defined mystique of communes, artists, and "dropouts." Armed with little but the name of one contact, I left in the summer of 1974 for the first of three one-month periods in Santa Fe.

My contact, a long-term resident of the area, provided me with the names of three people who fit my definition of a radical career changer. I had chosen three criteria to select a member of my sample: someone who had established a career of at least five years' duration before coming to Santa Fe; someone who had radically changed careers despite both lowered status and lower income; and someone who had taken a substantial financial risk in making his change, that is, who did not have an independent source of income that would allow him to choose not to work.

These first three people provided me with the names of others. Ultimately, I met and formally interviewed thirty-five people. Moreover, I also had many informal, chance encounters in Santa Fe bars, restaurants, shops, and homes that provided additional information and confirmation. Often just a simple mention of what I was doing led to new contacts and new stories. For example, while having a drink in a local bar, I described my research project to the bartender and was soon engaged in swapping tales with him (a former Broadway set designer with an M.A. from a major drama school) and another customer, formerly head of an advertising agency, now director of a local art gallery. Although candor was seldom a problem in my prearranged interviews, these informal encounters, which tended to occur in social groups, were richer than the more formal interchanges of two-person interviews.

There are a number of essential points to understand about my sample and the information I obtained. Radical career changers have no identifying signs of their past, no visible indices of their radical shift. I sought them out, in part, by creating them as a category of people. Of all the many decisions people make in their lives, I chose to focus upon one: the decision to change a career. With this focus, a group of disparate individuals suddenly cohered as a sample and were demarcated from other people who had not made this decision. In this sense, I partially created my subject matter.

They allowed me this possibility. My topic and background were acceptable to them. Also, they felt comfortable talking with me. They understood that I was not only a detached social scientist but also a person trying to understand his own life through exploring theirs. So the interviews must be seen in a context of our relationship, at a particular time not only in the radical career changers' lives, but in mine as well.

By understanding the relational and time contexts of the interviews, their quality becomes somewhat more intelligible. The overall direction of the interviews, whether formal or informal, was the same. I asked each person to try to remember the time that he was considering making his change and to tell me what had happened, and what he had thought and felt. I tried to enter his world and follow, through questioning and reflecting, the course of his decision, from "back home" to what he wanted for his future. Each interview was therefore open-ended in structure and unique in quality.

Some of the interviews have the tone of self-justification. This must be, since most of the people who were interviewed felt the need to defend their choice, a decision that friends and relations considered "crazy." Moreover, my desire to learn not only the "facts" of the decision but also the motives behind it may have contributed to this self-justifying tone.

What emerged were the stories of people ranging in age from thirty-two to sixty-two, with a mode around forty. All were well educated, holding at least an undergraduate degree, and many had postgraduate education. A broad range of former careers was represented: stockbroker, social services administrator, art school professor, social worker, television producer, and insurance salesman, among others—a range not unrepresentative of well-educated professionals and business people in any large metropolitan area. They had given up their professional careers for the narrow work options available in Santa Fe: construction worker, farmer, small-business owner, and employee in the extensive tourist industry.

Most of those I interviewed were men. As a man, I found it difficult to make a meaningful statement about the lives of women; moreover, I, and often the women I interviewed, were unclear about what constituted a career trajectory for them. The characteristic male path of schooling followed by work, seldom fundamentally disturbed by marriage or children, had been infrequently followed by the women I interviewed. With one exception, all had established careers that they had short-circuited upon marriage, or more usually upon the birth of a child. Some resumed working, often in a different career, after a number of years of being a wife and mother. The stories of two women are presented in this book to suggest the complex set of issues involved in a woman's life.

Each of the people studied had a unique reason for radical career change. Yet all shared a common set of core concerns. To best present these shared themes, I have selected the stories of thirteen people who speak most directly and clearly to them. These stories are presented as literary portraits rather than as quantified data or clinical description. The literary mode best conveys the richness and complexity of the issues involved. In the stories and the critical commentary that follows them, I have attempted to enter the frame of reference of the radical career changer, to view his life in his own terms. My own perspective provides the basis for the final chapter.

The material presented is now four years away from that initial conversation with Seymour Sarason. My dilemmas about work and meaning have been provisionally resolved. For this I owe a great debt to Santa Fe and the people I interviewed. While I still maintain a deep love for Santa Fe and continue relationships with some of the people I studied, I find now that Santa Fe is no longer vested with its former romance, of being a refuge, a place to solve my own dilemmas. What follows is a personal yet critical analysis of the lives of radical career changers, and to some extent, of my own life.

CRISIS

Santa Fe's tourist brochures are enticing. They display such offerings as "A Touch of Old Europe," "Indian Culture," "Fine Restaurants," "Skiing," "Hiking," and "Spectacular Scenery." For most of us, a stay in Santa Fe would be an exciting opportunity, a welcome break from the normal routine, a chance to meet new people and sample new experiences.

Yet for the radical career changer the same opportunity is a frightening one. He is not like the typical traveler, for he has no "normal routine" to break from, no home to return to. There is often no one to tell of his novel experiences, no one to view slides of how this world looked through a camera lens. Many of the threads of continuity that held his life together have been broken. There is not the same job to return to, nor the safety of the familiar, the social and physical environments have dramatically changed. Often there is not even the continuity of a marriage or a clear, defined sense of self. Santa Fe for the radical career changer is not an episode to be placed in brackets, separate from ongoing life somewhere else. It is his life, in a place where he must reestablish a new continuity from the fragments of his life back home. It is a life developing out of crisis, with Santa Fe providing the background and sometimes the means of resolution.

One of the roles Santa Fe plays in the radical career changer's life is dramatically portrayed in the following story. Here Santa Fe is seen as a refuge from a massive, almost total disruption of life back home. The crisis is ongoing, the resolution unclear. But Santa Fe provides a shelter where Chester can sort, examine, and reorganize the fragments of his former life.

9

Tick, Tock, Mickey Mouse

Chester's Story

There had been many silences in our conversation. Most were those fleeting, scarcely noticed, punctuating spaces that simply ask the listener to signal his engagement. Empty moments easily filled by tacit signs of interest and approval.

Then there were those longer silences, intervals while Chester groped for the right words or sometimes reached for beclouded memories. These spaces were more than commas in the conversation; they had an intensity drawn from looking inward. Silences asking for assistance without a suggestion of what was being searched for. They were comfortable silences, since he and I were still in touch, sharing the knowledge that the right word or memory would be found and that the silence was only a part of the rhythm of our conversation. A conversation, a line of words, telling the story of how and why Chester had given up a successful career in publishing to be a clock repairer in Santa Fe.

But the present silence, the one we were in the midst of, was different. Although it was a long silence, it was defined more by separation than by extent. Our eyes still met, but his gaze was inward—our contact only a matter of social form. He was searching for something, located somewhere far beyond the edge of that consciousness where fleeting words or memories reside. The rhythm of our conversation was now broken, and there was little hint of whether the search would end successfully, the silence broken, or whether the conversation would end in emptiness, the search too difficult, the idea too evanescent. But I sensed that the missing thought would be found and its description would provide a cap to the story now almost complete in its telling, the present being defined by an unspecified future.

Our conversation had begun with very few silences. Chester

answered my opening question about how he came to Santa Fe with a rapid-fire biographical account.

"I've always liked this place. I went to college, for a while, at the University of New Mexico, and my sister has lived here for seventeen years. I've visited a lot. But I hadn't been very responsive to it. I lived through other people's views, not my own. It's only when I needed a refuge, and that's what Santa Fe really is to me now, that I could see it for myself."

Chester had thrown out a lot of leads. I decided to follow the "refuge" idea first. "What was Santa Fe a refuge from?" I asked.

"I didn't know when I came out. And it's only becoming clearer now after almost a year. It seems that everything important I've done has been unconscious. It's as if the deeper part of my personality, my inner survival self, shoved the crew and captain aside and took over the ship and somehow kept me from running on the rocks. It forced me, over my better intellectual judgment, to do uncomfortable things, like coming here."

"What was it about 'here' that was so difficult?"

"I came here to see if I could live with myself. I've always lived in other people's views of me. And that wasn't working. I began realizing, all too slowly, that I had to find myself."

"What brought this awareness?"

"It was a lot of things coming together. But probably the most immediate thing was meeting my mistress. She was a projection of my anima. She embodied all those things I wanted to be but somehow couldn't believe were possible or even right for me. She is nineteen years younger than I. She's a free-lancer, a crazy, zany, inventive woman. An artist who works with her hands. We had an affair and I went to live with her in Ireland."

"For how long?"

A brief silence. "About seven or eight months. It was a wonderful experience," he continued, "but also deeply painful. I was being tortured, compelled unconsciously, by some psychic explosion, to combine the elements of her and me together. Through her, I could share vicariously in the life I wanted for myself, the impassioned, direct, hip, free-in-the-countryside style. I saw my own life, of being stable—middle class, of course—given to eccentricity, working in a job I increasingly hated, in a good, loving yet discontented marriage. These are the two parts of me that I'm trying to put together here."

"What was it about your life—the job, the marriage, the style—that wasn't satisfying?"

"I never really would admit it to myself. I was deeply unhappy. I saw it most clearly, at first, with my job. I was a science editor for a number of publishing houses. I got into it at the beginning of the paperback explosion. I had an unusual combination of skills—knowing science and being able to write. I enjoyed the work—that is, if they left me alone. But the industry started to change. There were more and more crazy deadlines. Then more and more demands for *esprit*, group consensus, corporate image stuff. Sort of being part of a machine. I was known as an eccentric, an oddball. But this didn't take off the pressure."

He paused for a moment—one of those fleeting, punctuating spaces.

"And I hated living in New York. I hated the socializing and the fact that I couldn't do things like shoot antique firearms in the city. Hell, I was earning a lot of money, and earning high grades for fulfilling everyone's expectations. But I wasn't happy."

"What did you do about it?"

"I kept in publishing but took lesser-paying jobs that promised more autonomy. It was a losing battle. Then I heard about a graduate program in public health at Yale. I applied and they courted me. I was so flattered. Imagine me at Yale when my headmaster at prep school had said that I would never even get to sweep the back stairs of an Ivy League school."

"Were you that poor a student?"

"It seemed fated that I be poor at everything. I was a rebellious and sickly student. I didn't even graduate from high school. I got, what do they call it?" Chester groped for the word. "Oh, sure, a transition certificate. I didn't do particularly well in college either. So you can imagine how important it was that I was doing well in editing, and then to think, being courted by Yale."

"How did Yale work out?"

"It was terrible. Graduate school takes one ball when you start and gives it back at the end, usually with a piece missing. After I finished I worked for a while in a public clinic. It wasn't very satisfying. Then the funding stopped. I could have gone up to the state level but I knew this would be more of the same. I hated the whole public relations operation."

"Is this what the graduate program trained you for? Wasn't this a shift in career?"

"Well, it wasn't supposed to be. I had learned these skills of ingratiating myself all during my life, and especially in publishing. But I hadn't expected my work in public health to be that. I was supposed to be using my writing and science skills, and I wasn't. I was a glorified fund raiser. I was becoming deeply despondent. I had just begun orienting myself toward myself. This is when I met my mistress."

"How did your wife take the affair?"

"She wasn't very happy about it. But given my deep unhappiness and her sincere love for me, she accepted it. She took me back when I returned from Ireland."

"Was your marriage a happy one?"

"We deeply loved each other. And still do. But the marriage represents a side of me, the socially acceptable part. And I live in conflict between that side, the face that pleases other people, and what I am learning is another part of me, a part I like better. That's what my mistress crystallized for me. And Santa Fe is the place to deal with these two warring parts."

"What did you do for a living after you came back from Ireland?"

"I gave up the whole public health thing and tried, somewhat unsuccessfully, to get work doing what I loved—repairing antique clocks. I would never let myself accept, until recently, that what I wanted, what I enjoyed, had any validity. I've always liked clocks, ever since I was very little. Then when I was wandering around Europe—let's see, that's when I was about twenty-two—I apprenticed myself to an antiquarian horologist in England. Crusty old man. He had single-handedly resurrected the industry. But I couldn't justify doing this kind of work as a career."

"Why not?"

"I always saw work as a way, an extension, of pleasing someone—parents, teachers. I felt I had to make this situation as comfortable as possible. Work was an exterior justification and never fulfilled me, except in the distraction. I felt this all the time, but I thought it was my lot to be unhappy and depressed. But I couldn't define it, or put a name on my problem." Another punctuating silence.

"You see, I was socialized to believe that anything I wanted was eccentric. I was always put down for what was me. I had a benevolently instrusive, overprotective mother who wanted me to fit suburbia's social definition. I spent most of my forty-nine years, until now, trying to do this. I never fit, and now I'm struggling to fir.. myself.

"All along, I had to create a secret life for myself. Somehow, in that world, I could only be a horologist if I were independently wealthy, a sort of country squire. When I came back from Ireland, I gave up that secret part and went public. I didn't have much success on the East Coast. I'm doing a bit better here."

"What were the risks for you in coming out to Santa Fe?"

"My wife's displeasure. Going off to Ireland was bad enough, but going off again, this time to Santa Fe, was too much. She instituted divorce proceedings. I'm terribly torn. I love my wife and children. I love my mistress. She wants me to come back to Ireland. I'm trying to put it together. It's been hard. I had a little money when I came out to exist on.

Now work is starting to come in and I might be able to survive."

"What have you found for yourself in Santa Fe? What does this refuge look like?"

"I find real support here. I find that people have been through somewhat the same things as I have, and often a lot more. They understand. That is very comforting—especially since I judge myself very harshly. I find that a lot of people here have confronted their loneliness and made it work. At times, I almost feel that I could enjoy living with myself. It is easy to fall into intimacy here, on all sorts of levels. But what I don't need now is another intense relationship."

Chester was speaking more slowly now. He was describing a new set of experiences, only partially assimilated, not well practiced in the telling. He was thinking out loud, trying in the silences to grasp an emerging, conflicting, and uncomfortable new self. I knew my next question was going to be difficult for him, but it seemed important. I asked, "Where do you see yourself going in the future?"

This is when the long silence began. I sensed Chester's withdrawal and, for the first time, became aware of the sounds of birds chirping in the patio—peaceful songs punctuated by the intrusive noise of motorbikes, trucks, and cars trying to climb the steep hill on the far side of the garden. The patio where we sat was recessed from the main street—a place of refuge from everyday life, Chester's haven from the world and parts of himself. My attention was brought back when I saw a subtle change in his eyes, a shifting of focus from inside to outside.

He said, very measuredly, "I've been doing a lot of thinking about that question." There was an agony in his face that presaged his next statement. "Where do I go from here? Where the hell does this all lead to? It's an obsessive question. Am I to be a sort of happy, eccentric clockmaker in Santa Fe, living in a little ole cabin in the mountains with lots of tick-tock, Mickey Mouse things?"

He looked toward me imploringly for an answer. I wanted to

look over my shoulder to see if anyone was there who could answer his question. We talked a while about philosophies of living, on a level of abstraction purposely missing the real point. The conversation ended soon afterward, with our shaking hands and promising to keep in touch.

Chester's crisis is near total. His former roles and ways of acting—high-status professional, husband and father—are not very adaptive. He has come to question their meaning, purpose, and value. Now his concept of self has begun to crumble.

For Chester, Santa Fe is the refuge where the disintegrating pieces of his life can be seen from a critical distance. By confronting his loneliness he hopes to reconstruct these fragments into a new, more meaningful whole.

But Santa Fe is not far enough away. He has brought the conflict and crisis with him. He is torn between the part of himself that accepts "other people's" views of the world and the "eccentric" part of his being. These two aspects have their real-world counterparts in his mother and wife on one side, his mistress on the other. While the external events of his life— radically changing careers, impending divorce, and the desires of his mistress—are all quite real, their significance for Chester lies in their being triggers, pressure points, that call forth their psychic counterparts. He has introjected the external realities by giving them internal reference. But even on this level, resolving them is problematic.

Chester had previously avoided crisis by accepting the traditional part of himself and suppressing to "a secret life" the other, eccentric part. Although he had long been aware that his work was not fulfilling, that his marriage was safe but not satisfying, he had sidestepped the crisis by assuming that this was his lot in life, to be "depressed and unhappy." His mistress set the crisis in motion by encouraging him to act out the suppressed side. Had he been secure in either image of himself, there would not have been a crisis of such proportion. He could have more readily accepted one of the alternatives and paid whatever price it exacted. But Chester could not resolve the dilemma; the conflict was too deep, the opponents too well matched. Nor could he deal with it at home; the pressures were too intense and close. He needed Santa Fe for the distance and aloneness it provided.

The most visible indicator of Chester's crisis was his radical career change. A human interest item would probably headline his situation as "Successful Science Editor Turns Clockmaker." Its stress would likely be on his former and present work life while muting his troubled home situation and his eccentricities. Such a presentation would create the impression that Chester's problem and radical decision were work-related. And this image is to a large extent true; Chester's life and identity had been defined by his work life.

But his crisis involved more than this. He had already tried to deal with his career by first redefining his science editing job, and when that effort was not successful, he retooled for a career in a seemingly unrelated area. Yet both solutions were still within the traditional "other people's" views of himself, and they did not work; the unhappiness and depression did not disappear. These changes in work couldn't produce a miraculous outcome since they never acknowledged the other part of Chester's self. His mistress made this point all too clear.

From the perspective of Santa Fe, Chester sees that his crisis of work was embedded in a more general issue, namely, the question "Who am I?" His decision to become a clockmaker did not resolve this question either. He still cannot accept as valid doing what he enjoys. He is oppressed with wondering whether being a clockmaker is what he is meant to be. In his self-analysis, he is questioning, at a fundamental level, not simply the issue of work but more generally the trajectory of his life and his sense of identity.

Yet there is a hidden answer in the way Chester's questioning is structured. The background voices of his mother, his wife, and "other people" seemed to be guiding his concerns. His final question does not have the affirmation of a correct decision. He does not ask "What purpose was I fulfilling by being a science editor?" Rather, the question is formulated in terms of whether being a clockmaker has any value. Value defined by what? Partially a cosmic perspective; his question asks about the meaning of life and the place of work in some grand yet unknowable design. Also, his question reflects a cultural, "other people" judgment. He feels their censure: being a clockmaker does not contribute as much to the social good, or carry the same status, as being a science editor. While he hoped to escape this indictment by going to Santa Fe, he finds himself acting as society's emissary, as its judge and jury.

This social point of view is underlined in Richard's story, a foil for Chester's. Richard is not a radical career changer. Far from it. His present work, however problematic, is at the core of his life. Nor does he want to come to Santa Fe. It is his wife who presses him to move. He does not perceive himself in crisis. His life seems sensible and clear. Although Richard does not fit the category of radical career changer, his story shows how the same setting and concerns can be interpreted in totally different ways.

Reversal

Richard's Story

I was sitting on the restuarant terrace, watching the tourists going by. Mostly I was waiting for an uncomfortable situation to materialize. The day before, one of my closest friends had asked me to meet with a couple she knew. I was to counsel the husband about the joys of resettling in Santa Fe. All I knew was that the wife, Sandy, loved Santa Fe and had somehow induced her husband, Richard, to buy a house in town. When they got back home to St. Louis, Sandy pressed her husband to give up his job. He was senior vice-president for a large corporation. She wanted him either to retire at the ripe old age of fifty-one or to find work in Santa Fe. They had plenty of money to live on, so there was actually no need for him to work. But Richard balked. He then insisted that they go to Santa Fe, supposedly for a vacation. The real reason for the trip was now becoming clear. Richard was trying to sell the house and thus put an end to all discussion about living in Santa Fe. Sandy was making a last-ditch attempt to sell him on Santa Fe. And I had the awkward role of "counselor to a reluctant husband."

My waiter came over, bringing another cup of coffee and a note with my name on it. Having never gotten a note in a restaurant, I flashed into a late-1930s movie scenario. A Viennese café. Sounds of violins in the background. Mischa Auer handing me a lightly scented note. His eyes subtly shift to the left. I look over. There is a mysterious, beautiful Marlene Dietrich glancing at me seductively through somewhat embarrassed eyes. I flashed out of the scenario when my waiter said a little brusquely that the couple on the other side of the terrace wanted to see me. I looked over and saw a hand waving above the crowd. It wasn't Marlene but Sandy with her husband. There was no need to read the note.

I arrived at the table and we began the usual "getting to know you" biographical display. This was the second marriage for both of them, each having lost a spouse. She had three grown children. One, a near-Ph.D., was farming in a small New Mexico mountain community. Another lived in an ashram in Boulder, and a third was searching for his guru in India. While her background was, to say the least, a little offbeat, his was straight and powerful. He had grown up poor in New York and, after battling his way through the navy, had fought his way up the corporate structure to reach his present position. He sat there, well tanned, alert, comfortable with wealth, and obviously nobody's fool.

I figured there was no point in being circumspect about my

mission. I opened by saying, "I understand you bought a house out here but are still living in St. Louis. That's a little curious since everyone would give his right arm to live out here."

Before Richard could answer, Sandy said, "Like that waitress last night was dying to live out here. Remember that crazy situation? Those are the kinds of things I love about Santa Fe. What happened was, we went into this bar to have a drink. At home you usually expect the same casual dialogue, like, 'Good evening. What may I bring you?' 'Beer in fine. What do you have on tap?' 'Coors and Schlitz.' 'I'll have a Coors.' Instead the waitress came over, sat down, and said, 'I'm in love with the dishwasher. We're going to get married even though he doesn't know it yet.' I playfully asked her if she knew what marriage was about. She answered, 'Oh, sure, I was married for eight years. That was OK for a while. Then I had a great affair for six years off and on.' I asked her what 'off and on' was like. She replied, 'He was an anthropologist in Guatemala and I used to go down there for a while. And that was cool until I apprenticed myself to a silversmith in Mexico and my boyfriend had to start commuting. So we gave it up. Long-distance love-making is a bad trip.'

"After talking for about an hour we finally got our beer. The whole situation was so terribly unpredictable. That's what's so exciting about Santa Fe."

Richard managed a fixed, pleasant smile throughout Sandy's monologue. When she had finished, he quietly said, "That's fine for you, but I don't find these situations particularly enjoyable. Admittedly, there are a lot of things I do like about Santa Fe, like skiing and hiking. But, on the overall, I'd go out of my mind here. What would I do with myself? I wouldn't have my work here, and that's what I really enjoy."

Sandy chided, "Since when do you love your work? You complain bitterly about it every day. It's always the same: complaining, followed by collapsing in front of the TV. Then a couple of drinks and dead silence. It takes you at least an hour to put yourself together again."

"Sandy, I've explained this over and over again. There is a lot of pressure on my job. I have a lot of responsibility. But I can make things happen. I'm almost my own boss and I feel in control of myself and what I am doing. It takes a lot out of you when you're negotiating millions of dollars and dealing with people all the time. But that's what I enjoy, what I love about my work. And I'm willing to pay the price of being tired and upset at the end of the day to accomplish this. I've struggled to get to this place and I'm not about to give it up for the entertainment some waitresses provide you with." A brief routine, obviously well practiced, ensued between Sandy and Richard: a superficially pleasant but barbed bickering seemed to help the marriage go around.

I tried to break the circle of argument by telling Richard about Harry Feld, a resident of Santa Fe who had worked through a problem similar to Richard's. Harry's story was a good choice since Richard had heard of him. They had over-lapping business interests. Harry couldn't be easily discounted. Richard's ready categories—most Santa Fe residents being either "has beens" or "incompetents"—didn't fit Harry very easily.

"Harry had an offer for his business that he couldn't refuse. He had a choice then. It was obviously a painful one. Should he take the money and reinvest it in another business and start building it up, as he did twenty years before? Or should he take and invest the money and quit working at fifty-two? The decision wouldn't have been so difficult had his wife not pressed him to retire."

At this line, Richard shot a knowing glance at Sandy. I continued, "He told me he was really frightened at the possibility of not working—he couldn't see what he could do with himself. His only burning desire besides work was to raise horses. But this wasn't a full-time occupation. His wife was insistent and he decided to give it a try. He figured that the house and land would at least be a good investment." I thought I might have scored a point there.

"For about five months Harry couldn't deal with himself.

Time seemed endless. Then somehow he got into his own tempo. Now he proudly points out, 'There is only one thing I must do today. That's groom the horses. And sometimes that takes all day. The rest is my own option.' He has started to become politically involved and is working on new business deals. Whether he is happy or not is hard to gauge, but he seems satisfied with the change."

Richard was listening very carefully. When I finished, he said, "That may be OK for Harry, but I couldn't lead such a life. For vacation it's fine. But for a life, the tempo would drive me crazy. Like take yesterday. We were on a major highway and two pickups were stopped facing each other. The two drivers were just sitting and chatting, Lord knows about what. Cars were backed up and these guys in the pickups were totally oblivious. This went on for about five minutes. What was so strange was that nobody got upset or started beeping. I enjoyed it. It was quaint. But I can't handle it as a full-time diet."

"I've thought a lot about the question of time out here," I answered. "It isn't that things have to work at such a slow pace, but you have the option to move as quickly or slowly as you like. Can you imagine wanting to drive thirty miles an hour on a St. Louis expressway? You have that option, but it isn't very real. You'd be blasted in no time. Out here you can go thirty if you want to or fifty-five if you want to. The option is real because the pressure is not there. You can pick any speed you want to live at. It's your choice."

"You may well be right," Richard said. "But let me be candid. The tempo is only one reason why I can't settle out here. The real issue is doing something important, something of value. And I don't think Harry is using his talents, and neither would I if I came here. There has to be something more to living than doing what you want to do."

It was obvious to me, and gradually dawning on Sandy, that Richard was not convinced. As we were saying goodbye, Sandy said with a note of resignation, "We have time to see what will happen. We'll go ahead and lease the house for a year. Won't we, dear? It's better than selling it."

Clearly Richard is very far from crisis. Except for his wife's intrusiveness about Santa Fe, life is relatively stable, continuous, and defined. Its purpose and meaning are centered in work. Here he feels a sense of accomplishment, control, and mission. For this, he is willing to pay the price of winding down after work, with its sullenness and drinking.

He keeps this meaning intact by drawing a sharp line between work and leisure. For him, Santa Fe is just a pleasant place to relax from living, an environment in which he recoups his energy from the drain of work. Richard has virtually equated work and living. Anything outside the equivalence, like Santa Fe, assumes value only if it enhances living (that is, work). Living does not occur in Santa Fe; it resides in St. Louis and at work.

By drawing another sharp line between Santa Fe's "has beens" and "incompetents," and people who do something more than just what they want to, Richard further sustains his vested meaning in work. His logic is straightforward. In his view, people like Harry Feld are not "using their talents," which means that they are not "working," which then implies that they are not truly "living."

His train of thought is airtight; the lines are clearly drawn. They provide him with an excellent insulation against an undefined emptiness whose presence he implied when he said, "I'd go out of my mind here. What would I do with myself?" It is likely the same emptiness I confronted when I lived out my fantasy of not working.

What is it that literally or metaphorically would drive Richard "crazy"? He probably does not know, nor does he care to find out. Some of its fearsome topography is suggested by Chester's situation.

Having made a radical career change, Chester is still not

sure whether clock repairing is just as much a "distraction" as was science editing or public health. Perhaps all work has no value, no ultimate meaning or purpose. Perhaps it is just as empty as the assumed void on the other side of work. Other aspects of living, like family, love, and physical surroundings are now seen as subtly interconnected with each other and with work. They too may be open to questioning, thus sharing the space of emptiness.

For Richard, the emptiness is defined by the absence of work and the lack of meaningful alternatives to make up for it. His work has always been his life. All other activities are relegated to the role of supporting actors in the central drama of career. If he allowed himself the awareness of how his life is, or could be, he might experience the interconnectedness of work with those relegated aspects of living. He might have to recognize that his clear distinctions may be arbitrary and without ultimate meaning. To confront the emptiness beyond work is to risk the awareness that work itself may be without ultimate meaning and cannot necessarily be equated with living. By defining his life into clear-cut, airtight categories he avoids the crisis that Chester and other radical career changers have experienced. But, as the radical career changer views it, there is a price to be paid for avoiding a crisis. The price is to live a life of partial, illusory meanings. An absence of crisis may not mean happiness but may rather indicate a perennial state of distress, which the individual uncritically accepts as a basic condition of living.

Through their crises, the radical career changers understood, largely in retrospect and often painfully, that such blunting of awareness does have an impact, however subtle. There were indicators of the problem—often a gnawing sense of dissatisfaction, sometimes compulsive spending, alcoholism, or marital disruption. But they did not allow themselves more than a fleeting awareness of their problematic situation. With the trigger of some event, like marital discord, or losing a job, or sometimes simply taking a fresh look, the radical career changers allowed themselves a critical examination of their lives. They now indict their friends "back home," people like Richard, for drawing artificial lines around their activities, for falsely investing total meaning in work, and for not having the courage to search for a more fulfilling life.

As the human interest items often imply and as our society usually views it, their way of finding a more meaningful life was to make a radical career change. But such a characterization of their solution is far too narrow. (A more appropriate term would be "radical life change," because changing careers was only a secondary outcome of searching for a better life in Santa Fe. But I shall stick to "radical career change" since it is more commonly used.) None of the people interviewed came to Santa Fe to pursue a particular career, whether as a desk clerk, construction worker, or school-bus driver. They all knew that they did not want to continue in their former careers and that they did not want to define their lives in terms of their careers. Santa Fe's narrow economic possibilities offered them little other option than to radically change their careers since they could not find employment equal to their former status or income. But they believed that the cost of lowered status and income would be offset by living in a setting where a meaningful life could be created.

Moreover, the fact that other areas of life were usually interconnected, in varying degrees, with their questioning of the meaning and value of work again indicates that the term "radical career change" is too narrow. The most common form of linkage was between work and marriage. In some cases, the decision to change careers also led to a reevaluation of the family situation. In other cases, the spouse's unwillingness to accept a change in career led to a deterioration in the marriage. The most general case was one in which a decaying marital situation interacted with and was an integral part of the crisis in the work sector.

There were other forms of interrelationships. For a thirty-seven-year-old social service administrator turned jack-of-all-trades and sometime welfare recipient, the unacceptable fund-raising aspect of his job might have been tolerable had it not intruded in his work life. The requirement to cater and pander to the agency's rich supporters created a number of problems for him. It invalidated his desire to create a service for those who needed it, those people who did not financially sustain the agency. So his work goals were frustrated. Also, in the course of creating an agency for his rich patrons, he became aware that his non-work life was taking on the cast of his patrons' lives. In giving up a career that had produced frustration and promised little better, he was also released from a life style that he found unacceptable. Or, for a fifty-five-year-old eminent television producer turned school-bus driver, the choice involved giving up an unacceptable future. The approaching slowdown in his work life, as he neared retirement, made his situation intolerable. He was willing to give up his successful career for the possible realization of his long-standing desire to work in the theater. Or, for a forty-two-year-old former art school professor turned dress designer and store owner, his job at first presented few problems. But his work satisfaction was being eroded by his difficulties in living in a city where he felt alienated and unsafe.

Whatever the form of crisis, it impelled psychic distance from the radical career changers' worn-out meanings and behaviors. Santa Fe offered the needed physical and psychic space from those meanings. In Santa Fe, they could examine their former lives and try to evolve more meaningful alternatives.

But why Santa Fe? There are a multitude of places where such a refuge could be found, where a new life could be sought. One part of the answer lies in this environment's physical and psychological openness. One major effect of this openness is that it allows a redefinition of the radical career changer's concept of self.

THE LIVING LANDSCAPE

Most people coming to Santa Fe are drawn to the landscape. It is powerful, compelling, and varied, a world whose starkness verges on the fearful; it also invites exploration and involvement.

For the average tourist the landscape is to be observed and used. It is a source of aesthetic pleasure. It is a setting for hiking and skiing. While the tourist is active in movement, he is passive in experience. He takes, receives this world, and then passes on to another landscape.

He sees little reason to engage the landscape in any more involved terms because this world is seen as inert and fixed, a painted backdrop to provide experience and to set the stage for his activities. He seldom recognizes that the physical land is active and living. Its movements elude him because the changes are subtle: the life of the landscape occurs in a time frame far beyond the person's brief experience. Nor does the tourist see the landscape in its human dimension. Within the seemingly inert setting are people living in relationship to it. There is a past, present, and future of living embedded within the geological frame of the land. The tourist often does not realize that he is also part of this ongoing life—his time frame is even shorter than that of those who have continuity in the landscape.

To experience the process of the land requires involvement and time. To comprehend the landscape's subtle meanings requires an effort that few people are willing to expend. If an individual does obtain an understanding, then he may see a different scale, another measure for his life, one far different from that provided by standard social definitions. This new definition may be, like the landscape, austere and frightening, yet drawing for a reevaluation of living.

Most radical career changers usually experience the environment in the same terms as the average tourist; although they have the continuity of living within the landscape, they generally experience it passively, simply as a setting for their own activities. A few, as represented in the next two stories, involve themselves more intensely in the living nature of this world. These people have chosen to live and confront themselves within the landscape. Here they search to define who they are.

The two landscapes presented in these stories are dramatically different. Mark's environment is the flatlands of the Indian world—dry, eroded, dusty. It is powerful in its rhythm, projected and assimilated in the incessant drumbeat of the ceremonial. Earth and man move in an indeterminate, synchronous tempo. Ron's landscape is the high mountains and green valleys of an isolated Spanish village. Here the world is powerful in its starkness, in its implied conflict between man and nature, man and man. Yet there is the common thread in both stories of a searching for self in relationship to the ongoing living scale and meanings of the landscape.

On the Road to Truchas

Ron's Story

The road kept climbing, constantly turning. The town of Chimayo nestled below among the gnarled sandstone. Another turn. There were the high Truchas peaks ahead, still glistening with snow in this bright, warm, early June day. Another turn. A stark wooden cross, black against the white snow, was no gentle shrine for quiet contemplation and reverence. There was too much anguish in the rough texture of the cross's wood, too much imploring in its soaring height. More climbing. Another turn. The glint of sunshine reflected as if in a thousand mirrors. Higher. Another turn and a gentle slope down. The tin roofs of Truchas reflecting the powerful sun. One last turn. The blinding glint of the tin-reflected sunlight shifts.

I park the car on the main street in front of a grocery store. No signs of the tourist world here. Two young men lounging in front of the store stare at me with curiosity but little warmth. I look around for a street sign. None in sight. And no streets, really, just alleys curling off the main road. I choose an alley and walk down the dirt path. Low, worn, tired houses, abandoned cars, rusting cans strewn haphazardly, and the white Cadillac, the "signpost" that Ron had mentioned. His house is two doors from the car.

I knocked on his door. I was greeted and ushered in by an ascetic-looking man somewhere in his late thirties. His clothes were well worn, like the beaten house and its sparse furniture.

I asked Ron about the white Cadillac. "Oh, that was mine," he answered. "All my savings were tied up in that car. I had driven out here from Boston and sold it to Bill Tate. He is the only one in town who could afford it. With the money I bought this house. Then I was on my own."

"How did you find Truchas? It certainly is off the beaten track."

"I had some friends who were going to school at the University of New Mexico. They wanted to get married in a beautiful, spiritually high place. I agreed to come out and perform the service. Their place was Truchas. When I got here I was drawn, almost pulled, by the landscape. Partly it was the sheer physical beauty. But that seemed to be the surface of the landscape. That's what my friends found so appealing, and it drew me too. But I knew there was something here, something more than a lovely landscape. I didn't know what was drawing me, but I knew I had to be here, to somehow get beneath the surface.

"This all happened at the right time in my life. I was becoming more and more disillusioned with my work. I found little fulfillment in it. I had gone into the ministry to help people, to be their counselor, to understand them and to experience things with them. What I found was hypocrisy among my parishioners and hypocrisy within the church. People were Christians only on Sunday. During the week they led lives that were immoral and unacceptable. They came to me for counseling so that somehow, in some miraculous way, I would take away the guilt and horror of their lives. But I couldn't do this. No person can do this. Only God can make them whole. But finding God was too much effort for them; they wanted me to be God, to be something more than a person. But how can anyone be something more than human?" He obviously didn't expect me to respond to his question since he continued, without pause, telling his story.

"Also I realized that going into the ministry was my way, and the best way I could find, to help people. That's been my mission ever since I was very young. Has it ever happened to you that you know something is right, you just know it in your soul without questioning or thinking about it? That's what happened to me when I was ten. My mission was shown to me by an episode with my father. One day, he and I were down by the river. There was a feeble old man there selling pop. He was pushing a cart and it tumbled over. There were a lot of people walking around but nobody stopped to help the man. And I felt that I didn't want to help him either. I was just a young kid at the time, but somehow I had already learned that helping people was a sign of weakness. My father went over and helped the man pick up the soda pop. Here was a respected businessman in the community, dressed in his Sunday best, kneeling to help this old man. I remember saying to myself that I wanted to help people just like my father did.

"I've never found much helping in the world. People are too busy acquiring wealth and material things. They never have enough distance from their lives to see where the world really is at. It's so obvious that they can see it; it's in human relationships and being in harmony with God. I had parishioners who would come in and tell me the story of their lives—very intimate details of the difficulties they were having in adjusting to the world. I would try to help them, and yet somehow I always felt that even though they had come for help, they didn't really want it. Somehow they were satisfied with their life, even thought it made them miserable. I wasn't supposed to help them—that's not what they wanted. They just wanted a seal of approval." There was anger and disgust in his voice.

"Ever since that episode with my father, I knew that God created us all, animals and plants and other living things, to live together. Yet man has managed to divorce himself from all this. And when I came out here to perform the wedding, I began to wonder whether I had fallen into the same trap. The landscape somehow told me, in a way warned me, that I might have lost touch with creation and myself. I felt dwarfed by the landscape; I was cut down to my right size. I decided to live here and find myself and, in the process, hopefully find my relationship with God.

"So I left my two churches. Oh, I was a very successful minister. I had lots of parishioners, a nice home to live in, and offers of bigger and better churches. After selling the car—the last vestige of my past life—I began learning how to survive. I spend most of my time keeping alive. I chop a lot of wood so that I can keep warm in the winter. I have lived through two already, and they are brutal. I spend a fair amount of time working in the garden so I can grew my own food. It's hard but I enjoy it. It's me that's living in the creation of food and warmth, not someone else producing it for me. When I run out of what little money I need, I work down below, flipping hamburgers. I hate that work, but it has to be done. In what time I have left after all this, I go walking in the woods. There I find the peace and solitude to think and read. I've also started writing about my experiences here. Maybe my writing will help people understand their lives. I become less and less sure that my ministry will serve that mission.

"Are you up to walking? I'd like to show you some of the places I live in—that is, the spiritual part of me."

We left the house and threaded our way through the alleys. Ron stopped before a small house, blank in appearance, with a large padlock. "This is a Penitente *morada*. It's kept very secret, but everyone around here knows that all the paraphernalia is in there—the death cart, the whips, the *santos*. Did you happen to notice that large cross on the way up? It's a Penitente cross. Although I've never seen the ceremony, they supposedly 'crucify' one of the brothers on the cross at Easter. They hang him with leather thongs and leave him there all day. All this at the end of forty days of flagellating each other with cactus whips. The brutality of living is a very real part of this landscape's meaning. I find it somehow exciting, on a primitive level. But I can't deal with it. I can't accept it. It is not my concept of man in relationship to God."

We moved on. "The people here reflect and live that harsh sense of the landscape. I have lived through a lot of primitiveness up here. About a year ago, for no apparent reason, my possessions—what few I had—were thrown into the gulley and my house was wrecked. Who knows why? They don't like Anglos up here. We practically need passports." There was again a note of anger in Ron's voice.

Truchas was now behind us. We started walking across undulating fields, heating in the blinding sunlight.

"I've been here two years now. I know I can live here, but I am seriously considering leaving. Physical survival is hard enough, but it's almost impossible without people around. The townspeople are hostile and the few Anglos that are up here don't have much sense of sharing and community. They are really only concerned about themselves. I've thought of moving nearer to Santa Fe—to a little town called Rowe. Do you know it? I understand there is more of a sense of sharing there. Most of the people are artists and craftsmen working in some form of cooperative. And they are Anglos; I think I'd feel more at home with them."

The fields had ended. We entered deep woods. In the distance I could hear the sound of rushing water. The woods opened into a narrow canyon. There was a careening river slicing the walls of rock. The stone glistened with the little light that could penetrate the chasm. Each ray was reflected, back and forth, by thousands of mica fragments in the rocks. Columns of stone hung precariously above our heads. Craggy boulders were strewn haphazardly along the path. The sound of water was deafening as the swollen stream fought through the debris of branches and rubble that blocked its course.

As we reached the river's fast-eddying pools and roaring cascades, Ron raised his voice above the noise: "My feelings about living out here are in this canyon. This place is beautiful. Yet that isn't the right word. What is the right word to describe a feeling of beauty that comes from harshness and brutality? This country is stunning. It draws you, elates with a power and violence that you know can consume you. Maybe it's part of our nature to be excited by what can destroy. I wonder about that a lot."

A Man of Solitude

Mark's Story

It was that hat. How I coveted it. A real symbol of being a mountain man—strong, independent, capable of living with himself. It was brown, deepened in shade by years of grime. Two brightly colored bird feathers soared in different directions from the headband ribbons. But what made it irresistible was the ragged hole in the crown. I imagined that it had been torn either by some passing arrows or by a hungry wild animal. The front and back brims, bent forward, created a continuous flow of movement with the tie band, worn Mexican style, across the back of the head. Unfortunately, the hat was not on display in a store. It was on Mark's head. I had tried to negotiate for the hat but with no success. It was as much a part of Mark as I wanted it to be a part of me.

His outfit was perfect. The hat, shading the dark sunglasses; the work shirt and pants; the relaxed body standing propped against the adobe wall. The guise said to the world that its owner had confronted his solitude.

We were at the corn dance at Santo Domingo. What a stunning sight—three hundred dancers and fifty singers, dancing in unison to an incessant, hypnotic drumbeat, pulsating with the chant of rattles. But it was the clowns who were at center stage. Their faces and bodies were dressed in white ash. Their heavy torsos moved constantly in and out among the dancers.

The next dance was just beginning. Mark was explaining the symbolism of the costumes and movements. He spoke in a slow, considered way—a straight line of feeling that seldom varied—a sense of solidity with a tinge of sadness. For Mark the dance was a world of infinite subtlety, what seemed to the uninitiated a scene of montonous repetition. Mark knew the Indian world; he had been adopted by an Indian family—a payment for persevering in "being around."

Mark suddenly stopped talking and I stopped listening—the scene in front of us had become transfigured. There were still the dancers and singers in the plaza. The clowns were still weaving through the lines. But the wind had come up, the bright sky had darkened, and an enormous cloud of dust enshrined the plaza. Through this fine gauze of unreality, the dancing moved into another dimension. And above the plaza, on top of the kiva, with its ladder extending heavenward, stood another line of clowns. They had magically appeared— their white faces and bodies floating above the cloud of dust. In a row, they looked like a long white sheet hovering against the angry sky. They seemed to be protecting the dancers, whose movements were encased in the shadows of dust.

The dancing continued. The sky cleared. The world returned to the expected. Mark and I left. We got into his VW bus, his home on and off for the past five years in New Mexico. He began telling me about his life of traveling. "I get about nine thousand dollars a year from my stocks. I only spend about twenty-five hundred. I don't need much. I live in the bus when I want to. Then I'm free to go. Each place is different. The whole rhythm of the earth changes in different places. The wind, the land, the plants, the sky. The Indians understand it. They live in it. That's what brought me to New Mexico. I wanted to be free to follow it, to comprehend what it's about. Come on, we'll go up to Santa Cruz lookout. I'll show you what I mean. I lived there for six months."

We jolted along the Nambe road. Mark punctuated our silence with information about the geological formations, the plant and animal life, and the shifting weather. It was a road I had traveled many times. It was always different. Each turn of the road unfolded a different facet of the landscape. The clouds and light called forth each part of the mosaic to take the lead. Sometimes it was the red of the course sandstone; sometimes it was the surreal shapes of the eroded cliffs or the massive green-to-black mountain peaks that served as their backdrop. Or sometimes it was the sky with its constantly shifting, moody clouds. At other times it was the silence that enveloped all. With Mark's tutoring the landscape was renewed in a different way. He said, as if reading my thoughts, "How can you get tired of this?"

He retreated into the landscape. A little while later, picking up the thread of his last statement, he said, "I've brought people up here to show them what New Mexico is all about. They're frightened of their souls. As long as they're in the car, it's OK. It's familiar. But when they get out, they can't handle it. I try to show them the rhythm of the land. It's so strong— you can't miss it. They are afraid of being alone with it. But mostly they're afraid of being alone with themselves. I probably shouldn't expect it from them. It took me a while to be able to deal with it."

Reaching the lookout, we walked out among the cacti to

an unexcavated Indian ruin. We sat on a mound and looked at the peaks extending in layers, one above another. Mark sat at attention, tuning in to every sound and sight. I was interested in the landscape, but most of my attention was centered on Mark's past. Although he seemed willing to talk about where he had been, he remained engaged in the landscape.

"I'd been coming out here since 1947. I made the decision to stay in '68, in just a couple of hours. It was at a time when my mind was quiet enough so I could listen to my heart. I was coming back from Esalen. I had been working with Fritz Perls and his people. I had to be back in Florida to run some groups. On the way I stopped in New Mexico. I decided then I had to be here. In this powerful landscape, I could be what I wanted and longed for in myself, what I wanted for my patients. Just to be myself, not what somebody else wanted me to be. But that meant a real risk. Not money, maybe losing friends. But really the risk was being alone. Alone with this landscape.

"My patients had that kernel of self in them. They would try to get to it. I would try to help them. But they were afraid of the risk. So they sucked on other people, on objects, to make themselves whole. They kept on showing up, trying to change. But they were always the same. There was too much danger in changing. That's why I gave up my practice. I wasn't very effective. Sure I was successful. I made a good living. But it wasn't accomplishing anything.

"So I went back briefly to Florida. Paid my bills, gave everything away—my books, records, all my possessions. I bought the VW bus and drove out here. Soon the bus got filled with other possessions, but they are from my life out here."

I thought of the sense of comfort, of enclosure, in Mark's bus. It was peopled with his objects, his life. A stuffed bird, some sea shells, Indian blankets, and books. Some of the books were about the birds, flowers, and geology of New Mexico. Others were strange and obscure treatises.

"Out here I'm free to do what I want. I read all the time. There is so much to learn. I move when I want to. And there is no one to tell me what to do, or to think I'm strange or doing something unacceptable."

The wind and the light had changed. Mark suggested that we move to a place where we could watch the lake. When we arrived, the lake was smooth, placid, but wind from an impending storm soon ruffled the surface. "I see my life as a series of stages," Mark said, "each one necessary for the next. It's like the lake. It's like the land. It grows and evolves with its own logic and its own time dimension. You know your place, your relative worth out here." He made a sweeping gesture to the mountains, the sky, and the land.

"I dropped out of high school. My parents, who are old New England stock, thought I was crazy when I took off to Europe and started a racing team. I was good. I reached the point of being one of the top racers in the world. Then I got drafted during the Korean War. They tested me and found that I was bright. So I learned Russian and had a top-secret job listening in on their radio communications. I needed to keep racing, to keep me and my cars in top shape. I tried to get a dispensation to race. No luck. I had four Ferraris sitting in the garage. I saved a lot of money during my racing period. That's what I lived on after I got out of the service and what I'm living on now.

"When I got out of the service, I couldn't get started again in racing. My cars had lost their fine edge and racing had become a tough grind. I decided to finish school, and I finally got an M.A. in psychology. I had the talent for it and liked it. But, like I said, after a while I realized I wasn't doing anybody any good, and not me, in particular.

"The place that I'm at is good. But I feel a need to do something of value. I applied to medical school. I want to be a doctor very badly. They said I was too old. So I'm applying for doctor's assistant training. If I get in, I'll start school in another year. It will be two years of grinding in the big city, but I can live with that. Then I'll probably come back out here and work around. I can be of value. Also, it'll be a hedge against the stock market falling." He smiled as if to justify his materialism.

We sat together for a while. Then I had to go home. Mark said he'd stay the night at the lookout. I wondered when I'd see him again. He floated through people's lives. I was sure that if I wanted to see him, he and his hat would be at some lookout or at an Indian dance. I had the strong feeling that we would meet again very shortly. I was right. I saw Mark, unexpectedly, a couple of nights later.

I was with a group of friends who had first introduced me to Mark. We were in the center of a very high evening. About midnight, we decided to look at the stars from the lookout. As we drove up, we wondered where Mark was.

We parked the car and started out in a mock search for him. To our total surprise, we saw a hunched figure sitting on a mound among the cacti, silhouetted against the mountains. It must be Mark, I thought. Who else would be wearing a hat in the middle of the night? The moon was full, the sky was spilling over with stars. All was silent. We walked across the field toward the motionless silhouette, as still as a boulder fixed in the endless landscape. When we reached him, he raised his head, took off his hat, and smiled—a smile that almost gratefully acknowledged our interruption of his solitude.

People have always escaped to the landscape to be refreshed by its quiet. Its sounds are more gentle, its rhythms more flowing, than the noises of everyday life. But most people have to return to the atonalities of "back home," leaving the landscape's sounds behind.

Ron and Mark have chosen, until recently, not to return from the landscape. They are searching beyond the surface sounds for a source of meaning that will inform and shape their lives. They listen with finely tuned ears. Mark hears, in the quiet of Santa Cruz lookout, the sounds of timeless change and the Indians' traditions and life. Ron hears, in the silence of the Truchas landscape, the disturbing sounds of his survival and the intrusiveness of people's brutality and unconcern.

For both, listening to the landscape's meaning demands solitude. It requires exposing themselves, shedding the familiar and examining existing answers. They must still the voices of the past with its possessions, commitments, and activities, so as to better hear the sounds of the landscape. The trappings of their former lives are too seductive and false. The meanings found in work, for example, they both see as empty. They were successful in work; they had more and more people to service. Yet they failed in that no one was helped.

Each stands almost naked in his solitude. Mark allows himself a few possessions but no fixed home. Ron stands alone without material or social support. In almost a self-crucifixion, he struggles to survive.

Now that kernel of self, unheard and unnoticed amid the noises of living, is seemingly exposed. What have they found?

They hear with greater clarity the voices back home—where they, and the people they attempted to help, spoke of changing but where they were truly unwilling and unable to confront their lives. Yet everything was measured against this unexamined standard; everything was dwarfed by its specter. This is a former self that should not be. For both Ron and Mark, the self that should be has a scale measured in the landscape's units; it is less knowing, less powerful than the former self, on a plane somewhere equal to the ongoing changes in the landscape. This sense of relative significance is more part of Mark's concept of self than it is of Ron's. Mark defines his life and its direction in the rhythmic terms of his world, ever changing, slowly progressing. He understands that he is only one member of a complex, ongoing life. While Ron accepts that his scale is less than the mountains and less than God, he has not fully accepted the unity in creation that he proclaims. He is humbled by his struggle for survival, yet he elevates himself above the primitiveness of the local people and the uncaring attitude of the Anglos. These people are somehow not part of unified creation. They are merely annoyances, voices that blur the clarity of the landscape's message. His search for self is too lyrical, his passion too godly, for him to accept that these intrusive noises are also part of the landscape, a meaningful part of that difficult-to-hear message. He is not aware that he is serving a self-imposed penance for his perceived failure in fulfilling his mission. His chopping wood, growing food, and flipping the abhorred hamburgers seems more human to him, more honest than the primitive penance of the Penitentes' flagellation. He does not see the parallel between his and the Penitentes' self-punishment. These primitive Christians are simply defined away as a part of the local color, to be experienced voyeuristically but not meaningfully.

Ron senses but retreats from the awareness that the Penitentes and the local people's brutality are really a part of him and of the landscape. He can admit an unacceptable excitement over the Penitentes' ritual; he can recognize that the canyon's beauty springs from its power and destructiveness. Yet he moves away from these glimmers of understanding by drawing a sharp line between himself and the rest of humanity. He is not part of their sin and brutality. He sits outside and judges the sinful, whether they are his former parishioners or, now, the local people. He hears the landscape's message, but in a partial, muted way. He deafens himself to the all-too-human voices that live within and around him. Ron's landscape is a spiritual one where God is to be sought and man is to be avoided.

Ron and Mark, while hearing different messages in their landscape, come to a similar end point. They both project emerging out of their solitude into a world of fuller human relationships. Ron wants to find community among the Anglos in Rowe; Mark hopes to be of service as a paramedic. Is their leaving solitude an escape from the values and meanings heard, or not heard, there? Or is the leaving based on a new understanding of self obtained in the landscape? There is more sense of positiveness in Mark's search for service than in Ron's return to the Anglo's world of the familiar, and away from the harshness of the Truchas life.

If Mark's solitude has worked for him, then he has moved into a new phase of the landscape's rhythm. This is one of the positive outcomes of loneliness and solitude, a state of being reputed to contain only terror. This fear of loneliness was well characterized by a thirty-five-year-old former art history teacher turned craftsman. She said, in discussing the isolation of her home: "I was pretty broke and living with friends when I heard about this place. Some professor owns it but he never comes out here. I took over the job of caretaker. For $25 a month it was a great chance. But those first few nights out here—wow, I'll never forget them. No cars, no lights, no people. Just me and loneliness. I had always been frightened by the fear of loneliness, so I never allowed myself the opportunity to really experience it. All my life people told me that loneliness was terrible. Being the kind of person I am, I couldn't believe the actuality of loneliness could be as bad as the anticipation. And I was right. Being alone is not easy. There are times that I wanted to run away from the terror. I was frightened by the emptiness. But the emptiness was me. Now I've grown to like living alone. It puts you in a whole different place in relation to the world. A position of real strength. I see people often and have lots of friends. But now I don't suck on the world to relieve my fear of being alone. I'm not scared of being by myself."

The landscape of her inner life, while initially frightening, is now satisfying. It can be filled, at her discretion, with friends, work, and other activities. By confronting the anticipation and the actuality of what appeared to be an emptiness beyond living, she found that it was not a void. It was as filled with meaning as the peopled landscape of everyday life.

The landscape of solitude is like all other landscapes, whether it be wild, rural, or urban. They are all realities in which an individual lives and has impact. The landscape is not a painted backdrop before which living occurs. Rather the individual is defined by and also defines his meanings in the world he perceives. The messages that are sought, whether in solitude or in community, in whatever landscape, are only partially produced by the mute geographical environment. It is for the human participant to interpret and create meaning from the voices of his landscape.

If the individual plays such an important role in creating meaning, than to what extent is a particular landscape important in defining self? One aspect of this question is illuminated in the next story.

The Presence

Max's Story

"Well, if you want to know the real reason for coming here, it's this." Max stopped unloading his kiln, placed his large body in a ramshackled, no longer overstuffed chair, and proceeded to tell a story he obviously enjoyed. "When I was seventeen—let's see, that was in 1949—I decided to see America. I was hitchhiking. One night I landed up in Santa Fe. I found this dance hall—it doesn't exist anymore. And there I met a very nice lady who danced with me for a while. Then she provided me with my introduction to the joys of manhood. I've always had a soft spot for this place ever since.

"In a sense, what I'm saying is that it really wasn't that important where I went. I just decided—it's now four years ago—that I had the option to do whatever I wanted. To go wherever I wanted. So I came here because this is where I first got laid.

"Why that thought—that I could do anything—came into

my mind, I have no idea. I remember the day vividly. There I was, deeply involved in my work, and this thought came to me. That I didn't have to be here sitting and working. I was a free agent. What was weird was that I was very happy doing what I was doing. I really kept that idea away from me, treated it with forceps, then examined it very closely. After a while, I accepted it as part of me. I didn't have to be Max the embryologist. I could be Max the anything. So I'm now Max the potter. It's really only me—Max."

There was a solidity to Max. Not so much because he completely filled the ragged chair, or because of his large, graying beard. He simply sat as if he were there and knew he was. His involvement was total, whether in our conversation; in emptying the kiln, which he was about to resume; or in selling pottery to the customers who had just walked in.

He returned from his sale saying, "These little planters go like crazy. I have this image that all of America will die of oxygen depletion from too many vines in too many hanging planters. And I have contributed to this mass suicide. I really like to sell them because I like to make money. I'm a potter but also I'm a businessman. I make to sell. I enjoy the problems of potting. I enjoy the doing. But I also like money.

"I took a financial risk coming out here. I came with ten thousand dollars in mortgage money and a small income. All of that money went for buying this place and fixing it up. You know, the small amenities like electricity, plumbing, heat. I had a very good job as a research embryologist in a big hospital. So now I'm a potter. What's strange is that I live as well on my income here as I lived on three times as much before I left. It's not a cost of living difference. It's just that I've redefined what's important.

"It's the same thing that happened when I decided to come out here. I had my Ph.D. for ten years and was well known in my specialty. I had a job where I was completely free to do whatever I wanted. I was approaching my dream of being internationally known and respected. I had a long string of

publications. I was invited to conferences all over the world—
Tokyo, Paris, London. But never in the U.S. I finally figured
that one out. But the most important thing was that I enjoyed
my research. It wasn't work—it was a life. I'm really work-
oriented. Here, I work even harder. I'm up at six and work
all the time. Potting is now my life.

"What made me start really entertaining that strange
thought was that my NSF money ran out. The hospital I
worked in offered me a regular position in medical research.
I was a bit aloof in those days, looked down at applied research. So I decided to try out that thought and shop around
for a new job in embryology. Would you believe it?—the best
I could do was some two-bit school in Florida. There were
plenty of jobs then; I just wasn't being accepted.

"I couldn't understand it. I knew I was good. Why couldn't
I get a decent job? My major adviser told me that a big shot
in the field had been asked for a recommendation by most of
the employers. He was submarining me by saying 'his sexual
behavior is extreme.' Where he got this from, I think, was
from some party where he overheard me say to my wife, 'Let's
split for the evening. That broad over there looks like a good
piece of ass.'

"Finding that out about being submarined crystallized a lot
of things. I saw my career in a new perspective. Like why I was
internationally recognized but had never been invited volun-
tarily to a conference in the States. Oh, I'd call and push my
way in, but they froze me out. I know I don't mince words. I
say what I mean. That doesn't make you very popular. But
yet my work was highly regarded. I enjoyed it. But my colleagues couldn't let me be.

"So four years ago, a couple of things were going. I couldn't
find a job I wanted, thanks to the submarine attack. I was
alienated from my colleagues. My second wife took off for a
whole set of reasons. I had no responsibility. So I took that
little thought, that I'm a free agent, and came out here.

"I decided to make my avocation a career. I had studied pottery for two years while I was in graduate school. I had a small electric kiln and a potter's wheel at home. And my second wife—she was an artist—really helped along. I knew I wasn't destined to be a great potter, but I could make nice stuff that would sell. And it does. I make enough now to live comfortably—by my new standards.

"What's fascinating to me is that I approach pottery with the same style as I did embryology. First, stages of precision and detail, then floating creativity with the intermediate outcomes, and then back to precision, trying to pull it together again. I'm beginning to realize how similar things are—pottery and embryology, back home and here. It's still me.

"I remember when I first came out I thought I'd be different. I got into the hippie culture and was tripping a lot on dope. Then one night, a flash hit me and I stopped. I was sitting on the floor with about ten people, getting stoned. I was feeling very high, grooving with the people. This was a nice place, I thought. People allowing other people to be. But then it hit me—I had the image of someone going up in flames, a giant immolation scene, and everyone would sit around saying, 'Man, do your trip.' I wasn't into not caring. A lot of kids are masquerading it as openness and tolerance. I care. I read everything. I care about the world situation. I work on a number of local projects. I'm involved. I was at home and I am here.

"New Mexico is a funny place. People here are more open and more accepting. But they are all detached from the world outside. Maybe this is because they cultivate themselves and relationships. But this seems to be at the price of being attached to the world. I try to do both."

Having been at Max's place over three hours, I knew he was a success at least in the interpersonal world. People constantly floated through—one lady to sell snow peas from her garden, another to work with Max's equipment, another simply to chat. Max always continued with his work but managed to be involved, attentive—a good listener. Always completely there. Max's place had the feeling of being a haven for people finding their way. And Max's presence projected the image that a path could be found.

"Who knows? I may go back to embryology. I saw an advertisement for a job as chairman of a biology department. I didn't get it because the money didn't come through. But I had all sorts of fantasies about going back. Even though I like what I'm doing now, I can foresee reaching a point where I'll want to go back. Then I will."

It was getting late and we had tickets for the opera. Max went off to change. Almost in an instant he emerged wearing a pair of slacks rather than his baggy white shorts, a silver concho belt holding up his large paunch, an Indian-design shirt instead of his ripped undershirt. His hands were now clean of clay and grime. Even his hair, what was left of it, and his beard, were combed. But he couldn't fool me or anybody else. I knew it was Max. And Max knew it was Max.

Max's landscape is simple—a potter's wheel and himself. The people who fill his world are only supporting actors, almost as incidental as the location of the pottery or even the activity of potting itself. Max's world is himself in relation to his work. His sense of self is strong and continuous even after the dramatic discontinuity of radically changing a career and an environment.

Max shows little of Ron's or Mark's purposive search for self. There is no need to explore; he brought himself on the trip. What explains the difference between Max's stability and Ron's and Mark's seeking? The most obvious answer is that Marx had a more defined concept of self before coming to Santa Fe. While this explanation is probably true, it masks the important point that Max's crisis never intruded on his self-concept. His problems back home were defined in terms of work. They were precipitated by the external circumstance of government funding, not by personal dissatisfaction or disillusionment. His inability to find an acceptable job never led him to question his ability as an embryologist or his personal adequacy. While his admitted directness and bluntness was, he believed, the basis for his colleagues' lack of acceptance and blocking his job access, he still values these apects of himself. Given that his crisis was perceived as one of external circumstance, it could be remedied by changing his career. This was the only point of yielding in the crisis: his colleagues' attitudes wouldn't change, nor would Max change his self-concept.

In contrast, while Ron's and Mark's crises also involved work, their work more deeply involved their self-concepts. Although Max's relationship to his subject matter was the impersonal stance of a scientist, the careers of both men involved working intimately with people through projecting aspects of themselves. They could have explained their failure to help as a fault of external institutional situations; or they could have localized the failure solely in their clients' unwillingness to confront themselves. Yet they saw that they had a part in this failure, that there was some undefined personal weakness in them that blocked effective helping. They also saw, in the reflection of their clients' problems, that they might also share in the same maladies. Their crisis was one of work only in a very limited sense. It truly was a crisis of self that found its form as a failure in work.

There is a more general issue raised by this explanation that should not be overlooked in the particulars of these three lives. It is the notion of the constancy of self-concept in the midst of changing landscapes. One side of the issue was graphically put by my friend Garry, a Pentecostal minister in Africa. During a sermon he was delivering in a back-country village in Kenya, he said, with a flourish of his arms: "We search for grace everywhere, but wherever you go Christ is always sitting on your shoulder. We just have to turn our heads to see him."

He was dismayed when his audience started looking over their shoulders.

Later Garry told me, "I'll have to change that metaphor. It is such a simple idea and so hard to get across. It's only partly language. The Africans are too literal. They don't understand English that well. But I have said the same thing to various Europeans and Americans. You know, the ones who wander the exotic route—Ethiopia, Kenya, India, and then Nepal. They think they are going to find salvation in these exotic places or in the consciousness of the primitive. They can't or maybe don't want to understand that they are the same person wherever they are. They carry themselves and Christ along with them everywhere. Grace is no further than a turn of the head, not in an exotic somewhere. I wish I could find the right words for my sermon."

Whether one accepts the theological tone of Garry's view or not, the message is clear—different place, same person. To search in an environment for a new self is senseless—we only find ourselves.

This continuity of self is very real in our experience. Witness the adolescent's often frantic attempt to construct an answer to "Who am I?" out of the fragments of his many-seeming masks. He is in search of a unity of self, a total identity that will organize the shards into a whole looking glass, a reflection of the total face that will not disappear with every glance. Living in a world of fluctuating interpersonal adjustments, of ever-changing environments, without a coherent image of self, would be like living in an endless fun house filled with constantly shifting, distorting mirrors, each of whose reflections would have equal validity.

Yet in our experience of self there is a seeming contradiction. Just as real as our sense of self-continuity is our experience, belief, or even hope, that a new self appears in new settings, that somehow a different place will make a different person. This experience of a changed self emerges most often on vacation. On holiday, we become different people because the restraints and supports of our non-vacation life are changed. There is no fixed schedule of working, no house that needs repairs, no oppressive budget.

We seek to encounter novel situations and people when we travel. We are willing to engage this novelty since it forms part of the excitement and freedom of a holiday. But we protect ourselves from too much novelty by traveling in the arms of American Express or by reminding ourselves that we will return, when the vacation is over, to the safety of the familiar. The sense of security allows, in turn, a great measure of freedom and independence to explore the new environment and ourselves within it. To the extent that we are willing to engage the novelty, on its own terms, we can experience the wonder of being different people in a different place.

The radical career changer was such a traveler when he decided to come to Santa Fe. What happened to his concept of self during the trip? At the point of decision to leave "back home," few of the radical career changers had any conscious desire to seek the experience of "different place—different person." To most of them, Santa Fe meant primarily an exit visa from the debilitating environment. They realized, often retrospectively, that they could have found, in their original settings, expression for themselves, even a community of people to share their concerns, and, less likely, independence within their careers. But their goals were not positively defined in coming to Santa Fe. Rather they sought an escape from what was wrong in their lives and a relief from crisis.

Nor was there any clear expectation of what the landscape of Santa Fe held for them. Their reasons for choosing this new landscape were seldom as frivolous as Max's explanation that it was the scene of his first sexual encounter. Yet most had only a vague sense, a tourist-brochure image, of what this new environment contained. The area had an appeal difficult to define: the physical landscape was seen as powerful, the people friendly, the cultures diverse. Santa Fe seemed a good place to live, or at least a better place than back home.

Upon arriving in Santa Fe, aspects of self had to change almost by definition. For a person seeking to escape a highly paid but stultifying career, Santa Fe's barren economic environment offered little possibility of recreating a former work world. Many noted, with a sense of wry pride, that New Mexico was one of the poorest states in the Union. In this sense, a person had to change or redefine one facet of himself, that aspect associated with work. Other aspects of self had to be modified—the world of the familiar was gone; former life style and relationships had to be reevaluated. New adaptations, if not new meanings, had to be established. The Santa Fe landscape had its own unique demands.

With the change from expectant traveler to local resident, many radical career changers experienced a strong sense of being freer, of feeling unconstrained by former roles and expectations. Virtually all found this new freedom and openness as powerful a defining feature of Santa Fe as the physical landscape. They described this freedom in varying ways: "People in Santa Fe do not stand on formality or judge you by material signs of success. You are accepted for what you are and not for what you have accomplished." Or, "People here are willing to accept all ranges of interests and values. I feel free to be and explore what I really am." The radical career changer felt that he could share his views about living and be supported, yet not be judged. There was a sense of community, a bonding based in shared experiences of life crises and shifts such as divorce, career change, and a reevaluated self-concept. These common experiences led to more fundamentally open communication about the problems of existence. A thirty-four-year-old former social worker turned construction worker clarified this point admirably: "This place is like a giant encounter group. We have all been through similar things. Just along this road, there are four of us; each one has changed his career. We share a common experience, so we can be open. We have all been through it, so there's no reason to be guarded. I don't live in the past or feel funny about it anymore, so I talk about it. But try and get my friends back home to talk meaningfully about their lives—you've got a good case."

It's not that the radical career changer spends a great deal of time discussing these issues; rather they are assumed as one basis for relationship, a common ground. Mutual, unspoken understanding is one of the key features of the radical career changer's feeling of being "at home," that place James Baldwin described as "where you don't have to talk about things everybody already knows."

The radical career changer's experienced sense of freedom to be himself suggests a way of resolving the seeming contradiction in experience, between self-continuity on the one hand and changing self on the other, with a change in landscape. Both experiences are simultaneously true. They avoid contradiction by a shift of emphasis in awareness. In the case of the radical career changer, he experiences a new and freer self in Santa Fe yet also recognizes that the same self existed in his former setting back home. It was only with a shift of landscape that the new sense of self, perhaps what Mark refers to as the "kernel of self," came to be truly experienced.

The role of the landscape, if it is experienced in its living form, is to highlight the different facets of that complex of traits too generally called our "self" of our "identity." Not that the environment creates different people; rather it allows certain facets to find freer, more open expression. This transaction between environment and self is like the light in the New Mexico mountains. The light calls forth first one and then another part of the landscape, making the environment appear constantly changing. Yet we know that the mountains, or in a parallel way, our inner selves, haven't disappeared or changed form. Another way to put the same idea is in the theological terms that Garry suggested. Christ may well be sitting on our shoulder, but he is easier to detect in some places than in others.

Santa Fe is thus not only a refuge from "back home" problems but also a setting where unique aspects of self are defined by their interactions with Santa Fe's living landscape. The one common facet that has changed for all radical career changers is the definition of self in relation to work. We shall next see how they define themselves in relation to their radical decision, where the usual role definitions in terms of work and career are no longer applicable, appropriate, or preferred.

DROPPING IN,
DROPPING OUT

Traveling is a very freeing experience. The tourist leaves behind not only his "back home" responsibilities but also his role definitions. In the new environment, it is not necessary to be a "high school principal" or "father" or "Elks Club president." These roles are traded in for the evanescent status of "tourist."

Like any role, the category of tourist has a set of expectations and constraints associated with it. But a tourist has a lot of latitude. While a high school principal back home would not consider getting drunk in a public place, he can, as a tourist, allow himself this indulgence. At home, he is known, defined, and limited by his place in the community. Here in the tourist world he is without roots, an unknown, anonymous person.

Nor do the local residents care to make his status less anonymous. They assume that the tourist is primarily concerned with observing, sometimes partaking of, but seldom being involved in the life of the community. Should he choose to enter this world in any meaningful way, he must give up the tourist role for the more differentiated responsibilities of "resident." If the traveler is intrusive, and yet refuses to accept the constraints of being a resident, he will be tolerated, in the short run, as a transient (it is hoped), insensitive boor.

To be released from former role definitions can be exhilarating. In his anonymity, and with the tolerant permission of the residents, the traveler is reasonably free to act and choose as he pleases. But this freedom can be enjoyed only when it is clear that he can return to his role definitions back home.

53

For all the constraints on behavior and choice that such definitions impose, they still provide a significant source of meaning, purpose, and embeddedness in living. Imagine a life in which an individual's primary definition was as a "tourist," an anonymous name on a hotel register.

Such a possibility existed briefly in the life of the radical career changer. At least in the area of work, and often in relation to family, he had no role definitions to return to. They were no longer valid or acceptable. Until he acquired new definitions in the Santa Fe environment, he would remain a "tourist."

But the new roles he could look forward to acquiring, particularly in the area of work, were only slightly more acceptable than being a tourist. It was difficult to take on the definition of "welfare recipient" or "waiter" or "school bus driver," given his past self-definition. Yet he could not maintain his former role as "social service administrator" or "embryologist" or "professor" in the Santa Fe environment. It was no longer applicable. Moreover, to publicize his former activities would lead to the role definition of "dropout," a category that the radical career changer bristles at. He wasn't a dropout hippie, one of those self-indulgent, uncommitted vagabonds. Nor was he a dropout failure, someone who couldn't make a go of it back home.

The radical career changer is thus faced with the difficult problem of definition. He is not a tourist. He is not what he was back home. He is not a dropout. Yet he cannot readily accept the expectations associated with his new, lower-status work role. Then how does he define himself? He often chooses, when pushed for a definition, to use the term "dropin" as a foil to the role of "dropout."

While all the stories in this book speak to the meaning of "dropping in," the ones in this chapter clarify one important relationship implied by the term, namely, that of the radical career changer to the dropout hippie.

The opening story provides a picture of a radical career changer's sources of self-definition. The attitudes of the hippies around him and the ambivalent voices of the people back home provide Len a basis for accepting and often elevating his solution to the dilemmas of "back home."

Commuting

Len's Story

"This all began innocently enough. About eight years ago, my wife Vera and I were on vacation, 'doing the West,' and fell in love with northern New Mexico. It was such a beautiful place and so open. Not only the land but the people. We kept coming back every summer. Finally, about three years ago, we decided, what the hell, let's make our vacation place our home." Len stopped momentarily to eat some of his breakfast.

He continued almost in midbite. "We had all sorts of schemes. Our first idea was to start an art school. We had made arrangements with established schools to give credits, but we ran out of money. Our second scheme was to build a solar house that would be sufficiently low in cost that poor people could afford it. It was a damned good idea, but unfortunately we got ninety percent finished and then ran out of money. Then we found this ghost town and this house and decided that we would try to do something together. Since we're both good with fabrics and we knew we could do a good job at it, we opened up a dress shop. Being a bit insecure about the idea, we brought in other people's work on consignment and had a sort of gallery. At one point we were so hard up that when a traveling salesman came through and had a good deal on sunglasses, we even put them out. They didn't sell too well. You want a free pair? They're just taking up space.

"What made us feel good was that our customers kept liking our stuff better than the stuff on consignment. So we gave up that part of it and went into the dressmaking business.

"But I was afraid to give up the old life. I couldn't totally let go of the security from my job. And at home I was somebody—Len Osmond, tenured professor of art at the Design Institute. Out here I was a struggling nobody. And we were almost broke from the solar house and the art school schemes. So what I did—it's hard to believe now—I commuted back and forth once a week to my job, a good fifteen hundred miles. I did that for two years. I finally gave up the 'jet set' trip two weeks ago. Thank God. It gave me great pleasure to resign my job, and with it went security and . . ."

Len paused as his wife brought in a tray of food. ". . . security and bagels. Sorry for the flip, but these bagels are precious—they were imported from the big world out there. I really thought at one point about opening up a bagel factory here. I am sure it would go over really big. It was funny. When I was thinking about that, some fellow from New York, who had worked for a paper there, wrote a beautiful article about what he liked about Santa Fe. He complained that the only drawback was that there were no bagels. That's my only complaint too." There was a note of wryness in Len's tone. "I found out that after the article appeared in New York, he had three long-distance phone calls from delicatessens in Albuquerque saying that their bagels were as good as anybody's, and four invitations to visit people's homes in Santa Fe to eat homemade bagels. There must be a lot of home-grown bagels all over northern New Mexico. With a continuous supply of good bagels, my satisfaction would be complete.

"Anyway, I gave up security and a lousy life style and acquired poverty. We wanted to settle out here permanently. When the first two ideas didn't pan out and we were pretty low on money, we decided that I'd keep my job. It was a bit tiring, but it kept us fed. I didn't want to be like everyone else in this ghost town, being on food stamps. This isn't our way of doing things.

"This town is a very strange place. Everyone here lives on the periphery of everything. It's an extension of Haight-

Ashbury. Most of the kids came out here, settled in the old broken-down mining houses, which are very cheap to rent, and tried to pick up jobs. But most of the time they live on relief and food stamps. They're really a nice group of kids. Some of our seamstresses come from the local area. But they come and go. This creates a funny atmosphere in town—a curious place to live.

"We wanted to buy this shop, but you'd have to buy the whole town—all the houses, the mine, everything, because of some stupid state law. I'm just not about to acquire a ghost town. I'm lucky if I can stay alive.

"But things are looking up. We've been doing a pretty good business even though we're off the beaten track. Actually, being out of the way provides one of our real draws—particularly for the tourists during the summer. You know, take the exciting back road, see the ghosts and the freaks, and surprise of surprises—a snazzy dress shop. We make a good product and we're becoming better known. I just decided that it was enough to do this job full time rather than commute back and forth and try to keep our lives together. I think we'll make it, at least I hope so."

Vera called from the work room: "You'd better get going. Remember, we have a fashion show at the Silver Dollar, and they need some more dresses." Len jumped up, gulped some more food, grabbed up some dresses, and said, "Come on along. We have a show at the nearby saloon. We can talk some more when I finish."

As we left, I realized how incongruous Len's shop was. It wasn't the building—it was only slightly more erect than the surrounding miners' houses. It was Len's dresses hanging on display in the window that belonged to another world. Here in the midst of the decay of a former time were these vital, organic objects, dresses flashing bright reds, blues, and warm earth tones against the drabness of struggle and erosion and ending, pennants reflecting gay colors against dying houses in an ominous landscape.

We soon arrived at our destination, another ghost town

about twenty miles away. This place also had its incongruity. While it was a little more sophisticated in its ruin, it still had the sense of returning to the land. Except for the bar-restaurant where Len's fashion show was being held. It was a late-nineteenth-century saloon, shining and bright from being well tended, and joyous from its overflowing crowd. Heightening this sense even more was a well-coifed, beautiful model walking around looking very fashionable and chic in a Len creation.

Len dropped off his dresses. We ordered a drink and talked some more.

"I really liked my job—not all of it but most of it. But I felt constrained by everything that surrounded it. When I got my M.F.A., I had a choice of a lot of different places. I decided to take this job even though it paid half the salary. What it gave me was the freedom to be and do as I wanted to. But the city drove me crazy. I just got tired of doing the same thing. I remember that one day I got up being sick and tired of going on the el. So I walked down to work even though it was thirteen miles. It was just a way to relieve the constant sameness of the city. What really drove us both up the wall was that we didn't have the freedom to do what we wanted. There were places that were unsafe, that said, 'Don't come here.' There were things that we couldn't do. We never felt completely free. What I always wanted to do was something that was creative—something with my hands. My father, in 1948, could still build his own house out in the suburbs. But now, he'd never think to do that. I'll bet there's probably a law against it. There were lots of things that I wanted to do, yet somehow they never seemed right to do in the city. Out here everything goes.

"This is a community that has always been open. The artists came out here in the twenties and thirties and settled in Taos and Santa Fe. What seemed like weird behavior back home was just plain normal here. Everyone else was doing strange things.

"People don't care who you are, but rather what you are. People are friendly and almost everything goes. I have all sorts of dreams that I want to play out—things that I want to create, things that I want to do with my hands. After I finish with the dress thing, if that's successful, I may do some other thing like build some solar houses or design furniture. Everything is possible and everyone around here is willing to go along with you, even work with you on an idea. There's a real sense of community out here, but it doesn't become oppressive. That's the nice thing about living in a ghost town. There are people around, either in town or nearby, and there's lots of visiting. But if you want to be by yourself you can easily get away from people."

Three drinks gone. Noise level getting intense. Len's rapid-fire conversation almost inaudible. Peace and quiet evaporating. "Let's go," Len called above the noise. "I can't hear myself think, and you look a little green."

As we drove back to the dress shop, Len ruminated about whether he was crazy for pulling out of things. "When I was commuting back and forth to my job, people kept on giving me double messages. On one hand, they kept on saying I was crazy to pull out and give up a secure position for something as fly-by-night as a dress shop. On the other hand, they kept on saying that they really wished they could do it. Do you realize that we've had more people here for dinner from the city than we ever had when we lived there? They keep on coming out to check and see if pulling out works. The only way they can know is by taking the risk. I've tried the commuting thing. It just doesn't work.

"I've thought a lot about that commuting. What I think is that there are two kinds of suicide. The first kind would be too much for me to take—the kind of slow death that people live when their options and their freedom are restricted. This is the safe, secure alternative, but it's deadly. I figured I'd try the second one—go for broke. If I was going to kill myself, I'd do it the other way, in one quick stroke. Luckily, things are working out. Even though I didn't mind commuting back to work, I realized that I had to make the break. I had to just pull out."

Arriving at the front of the shop, Len got out in his usual flurry of activity. I said goodbye since I had another appointment, a meeting with a full-time commuter. Although Santa Fe had many people who had made a break from their former lives, there were even more people who were checking out the possibility, wanting to make the break, to come out for good. But they were stuck in the limbo of commuting over long distances, and the even longer space between security and the possibility of a better life.

There is a veiled condescension in Len's attitude toward the local hippies. His visiting friends from "back home" also received the same treatment. For whatever the difference between the hippies and his friends, Len sees them as sharing the common fault of being unable to commit themselves to living in Santa Fe. The hippies come and go mysteriously; the friends keep traveling through, checking out Santa Fe's possibilities. Both must remain marginal to the life in Santa Fe; as Len came to see, one cannot commute in and out of living.

Len's choice of commuting back to work was dictated by the real economic risks in Santa Fe and his fear of insecurity. He couldn't accept the hippies' solution to economic marginality, that of picking up jobs and living on welfare. This wasn't his "way of doing things." Being on welfare goes against his strong work ethic, which says people should be independent and "make a go" of things, no matter how difficult.

Len was in a relatively unique position among the radical career changers in having a job back home to sustain his income. A job, moreover, that had a sufficiently open-ended schedule that allowed him to commute fifteen hundred miles to fulfill his responsibilities. Most radical career changers were not so fortunate. Applying for welfare was often the only way to supplement a meager income in Santa Fe.

Accepting a dole was difficult for them. Here were people who had been established in a career and accustomed to a high standard of living, now sharing in the world of the poor, unemployed, and marginal. This situation is presented in the following statement of a former social service administrator turned welfare recipient and jack-of-all-trades: "I learned a lot about welfare and food stamps in the first couple of months we were here. They really make it hard for you to be on food stamps. It would cost me so much gas and so much time that I finally figured out that it was better to try to get any kind of work no matter how bad it was rather than spend all that effort and money trying to get help. I felt like a failure the first time I went, especially at the point when they asked me about my level of education. But it was really funny, I was sitting there feeling uncomfortable and got in a conversation with a guy. He was even better than I was. He had a Ph.D."

This sense of shame and uncertainty about the future is an important component of what keeps Len's friends from settling in Santa Fe. The same factors kept Len commuting back to work. But he finally took the total risk because he recognized that living between two worlds made him a transient in both.

Fortunately for Len, the economic risk has lessened with the success of the business. As a reward for that risk, Len has "dropped in" to an important set of values that were seemingly not open to him back home. He feels satisfied with his product and his business. He feels unconstrained by the physical environment. His projects of solar housing and furniture building are sustained by the psychological supports in his environment. This openness is expressed by the history of the artists in the area as well as by a sense of community in the immediate vicinity. Here were people willing to accept and share in his activities and yet be nonintrusive. But the possibility of realizing these positive values could only come, as

Len sees it, with the willingness to take the risk of total economic failure and a total involvement in the Santa Fe environment.

But what does this commitment involve? His commitment is clearly more intense and complete than that of the hippies or his "back home" friends. But his affiliation is primarily to his personal goal of surviving and living in Santa Fe. The issues involved in such a personal orientation are developed in the next story, where a broader range of commitments is evaluated. Here Steven comes to examine his conflicting responsibilities, trying to resolve a difficult dilemma between personal and idealistic values.

A Dream Too Real

Steven's Story

We were in a holiday mood as we set out on the hour-and-a-half drive from Santa Fe to the communal farm near Canyoncito. Steven and I were in the front seat; his wife, Rose, was in the back, feeling uncomfortable. She was still recovering from a serious operation.

Steven constantly checked on how Rose was doing. His concern was informed by empathy. Gettin old, he had told me, meant becoming painfully aware of your body. Rose's illness had reminded him that he was almost seventy. Getting old. But he wasn't feeling old. Everything was working fine, at least well enough that he could go ahead with his projects. As I looked across at him, I saw a man bent by time with a spirit kept erect by a profound involvement in living.

We started talking about the coffeehouse they had had in Canyoncito. Even with its obscurity of location, Steven told me, it had been the crossroads for many young people going west to Haight-Ashbury and their later movement east to New Mexico and other locations in the Southwest. But soon our discussion somehow evaporated. The day was too clear and bright for anything but a holiday, the landscape far too beautiful and obtrusive for sustained discussion. We were off on a "trip," like kids let out of school for an excursion to the Statue of Liberty.

We kept on stopping to visit one person and then another. Steven and Rose had many friends who loved them and wanted to see them. After three hours of halting progress, Steven announced, "We've arrived. This is Canyoncito." In front of us was a row of small stores straddling both sides of the road. Some small homes were haphazardly strewn behind them.

"I always marvel at how little this town has changed since we came here," Rose said. "The same two grocery stores, the same gas station, and the same post office. The only new thing, and it's not that new anymore, is our coffeehouse. There it is coming up on the right. Steven, do you remember how upset I used to get when business was too good? I complained because I didn't have time to sit and visit."

Steven nodded absently and said to me, "The coffeehouse was really Rose's life here. We started it because we needed to survive. We couldn't make it just from farming. Also we felt the town needed something, and we thought it was a place to meet and relax. We wanted to do something for the people. They had been so kind to us. We sold it last year. It was about the right time to give it up. And with Rose being sick, we had to live closer to medical facilities."

"I really wish we didn't have to live in Santa Fe," Rose said, as if to herself. "It's like living in suburbia, Southwest style. It wasn't like that when we came out. Then, there was a sense of community, a real sharing. And it was tied to a sense of the land. There was wood to be chopped, cattle to be slaughtered, the weather to be watched. This brought people together. And the scale was right then." As I listened, I felt that she was in the midst of a well-rehearsed lecture. "Did you know that Steven was first oboist in the Santa Fe orchestra?

Actually he was the only oboist in town for a long time." Rose affectionately mussed Steven's hair. "Now people are isolated. It's not only because the town has grown but more it's that people will accept and actually want Colonel Sanders, or somebody else, to impersonally satisfy all their needs. Santa Fe is just a pretty painted movie set for the same old bad ecology."

"Rose is right. I really wonder whether the people you've talked to have made a radical change. I think their change is well intentioned, but it isn't extreme enough. One of my friends called what they've done 'New Mexico Chic.' You get some cowboy boots, a four-wheel drive, and some turquoise and think you've changed your life. But they are still tied to the umbilical cord of civilization. They still use wasteful sources of energy, consume impersonal services, and don't have a real sense of community or of the land. And the influences that make them not see or understand are so subtle and so strong that people can't see outside of the sameness of their styles. Really it's the same style that they had back in Chicago or New York, only with different trappings."

"Steven, tell Dave about the little girl who came to visit. Remember her and the chair you made?"

"That's a really good illustration of what I was saying. A friend came to visit with her ten-year-old daughter. We were about to sit down for some tea and the little girl just wouldn't sit down. I asked her why, but she wouldn't answer me. She looked sheepishly at her mother and then whispered something in her ear. He mother looked a little puzzled, started laughing, and then told us that . . ."

"Would you believe," Rose interrupted, "that the little girl thought the chair was dirty? It was perfectly clean. But we realized that the child had mistaken the rough-hewn, textured quality of the chair for dirt. Can you imagine a life with no textures? Kids are growing up in a smooth world, where everything is made out of plastic formica."

Steven suddenly stopped the car. He jumped out and called

after a figure that had just turned into an alley between two shops. "That must be Raoul Mendoza," Rose said. "Steven has been trying to catch him for weeks. He's the ranger in the area, and Steven has to check out some building plans with him. He's such a lovely man. He was so kind to us when we arrived in town.

"We actually found Canyoncito by accident. Just exploring the back roads. And in 1949 those roads were not to be believed. As soon as we saw it, we somehow knew that this was the place. It met all our specifications. Steven and I had drawn up a list of what we wanted before we left to explore the West. Canyoncito had everything. It was beautiful—that was the first item on the list. It also had a village economy, and it had farmable valley land. We asked around about available property. Nobody knew anything or would tell us what they knew. They thought we were crazy. We later found out there had never been any Anglos in town. And no new people had settled here since 1924. Fortunately we met Raoul and he told us about the Petrero—that's our farm. It's real name is longer. It means 'a gentle place where a young horse can graze.' An elderly couple lived on it then. They wanted to move into town because the work had become too hard and their children didn't want the land. The kids wanted the great American dream—imagine, to live in Albuquerque in a prefab house. And here we came, crazy gringos wanting to farm and learn how to build with adobe, and know all the things that their children wanted to escape from.

"Steven and I knew it was the right place for us. We were sure, dead certain, after that first night. We camped by a stream near the Petrero. It must have been about one A.M. when something happened. I'm sure it was a heaven-sent sign. Now this may sound like a movie scenario, but it really did happen. We were awakened by a noise—a distant, rhythmical sound. We couldn't place it. It kept getting louder and louder. And then we saw a horseman coming down the hill in the moonlight, singing a Spanish ballad. It was so lovely and mystical. Finding out later that it was only Mad Miguel didn't spoil it for us."

Steven returned to the car. "Raoul said that the plans are OK." We started out again, soon turning off the main road onto a rutted dirt path just outside of town.

"Steven, I was telling Dave about our first night on the Petrero. Wasn't it beautiful?"

"That was a very special night. Our dream had come true. Actually, it was my second try at the dream; it was Rose's first. I had tried it before in the Everglades with my first wife. We worked to create a new life, a style of living that was in balance with nature. But then the government started burning the Everglades, and no matter how hard we fought, it was a losing battle. We had to move out. My wife died soon afterwards."

"Steven and I met," Rose chimed in, "about a year later. It was in Jersey City, which Steven called the cesspool of the universe."

Steven chuckled. "I obviously wasn't very fond of Jersey City. But that's where I had to work. I worked for a big city planning and architecture firm. I enjoyed the job, but it was still work. Like all the jobs I've had, it had to be done to sustain life. But I never made my life my work. It was always temporary. Like the future is also temporary. But many people think, incorrectly, that work provides security. I keep my needs for money at a minimum. All the rest, the environment takes care of without payment. And I know that I can make money if I have to. Even now, in my 'advanced years,' money comes in without too much effort—mostly from lecturing and consulting. We've accumulated some money. It's tied up in the Petrero. But that's fine, since our dream provides us all the security we need. The money and the land make the dream possible. Do you understand?

"I guess I've never taken the Establishment very seriously. I dropped out of college because of that attitude. And I've always been suspicious of any government do-gooding, like

burning the Everglades. It was my uncle—a remarkable man—
who instilled this attitude in me. He was a Fabian socialist.
He always said, 'Never trust anything organized.' "

"But Steven, don't give Dave the impression that you were
a nobody. The work you were doing was very important, top-
level stuff."

"That's true, Rose," Steven said absently. He continued
with his earlier thought. "Anyway, when the company started
building facilities for wartime use, I quit. Rose and I realized
that it was the right moment to try the dream again."

"How did you pick New Mexico?" I asked.

"Haven't you read Steven's articles?" Rose asked in mild
disbelief. "He's been studying northern New Mexico for years.
All of his findings and thinking are in those articles. Steven
says this is one of the few ecologically salvageable places in the
country."

"Well, that was partly it, Rose. I've always loved New
Mexico, ever since I was seventeen. It was my first trip out
here. I had come to visit my uncle—a different uncle. Another
very unusual man. My God, that's almost fifty years ago. He
took me camping along the Pecos. The land was pure, the
country so beautiful and so harmoniously balanced. New
Mexico has been in my thoughts ever since."

Steven pulled off the road and stopped in front of a hut
made of sod and adobe. "Here we are. This is the Petrero.
This was the original farm building." As we got out of the
car, Steven stood very erect, pointed to the bustle of activity
on the land in front of us. He said with a big smile, "This is
the beginning of the commune. Hopefully, by this time next
year we'll be ready to settle permanently."

I looked out over the gently rolling land dotted by growing
buildings and busy, energetic people. "There are about forty
people working here now," Steven pointed out. "My friend
from the University of Minnesota brought out about ten of
his students to work on the project. The rest are kids—well, I
guess not really kids—they're mostly in their late twenties and

early thirties. They're committed to developing a new ecological relationship with the environment."

I started to ask Steven about this new ecology when a young
man came over. He was having a problem with angling a solar
collector and needed Steven's help. Steven said, "I'll be gone
for a little while. Why don't you read this grant proposal?
It'll probably answer a lot of your questions. My friend from
Minnesota and I put it together to set out our ideas. We hope
we can get some government support."

Rose went off to help prepare lunch. I sat down and began
reading. The proposal was filled with a lot of technical information about the use of solar heating and runoff irrigation,
much of which I didn't understand. The philosophy, however,
was quite clear. What Steven was arguing for was the use of
immediately available nonwasteful sources of energy—wind,
water, and sun—as a basis for a new ecological relationship
between man and the environment. This position was well
documented. He was also arguing for a new social form, a sense
of community, on a village scale, that would evolve from an
intimacy with the environment. This perspective was not so
well developed. How such a community would evolve, grow,
or sustain itself was left to some vague statements, often plati-
tudes, which in essence said, "It will take care of itself."

When Steven returned, I asked him about the proposal's
vagueness on the social and psychological aspects of community. He said, "There is no way to control people. Rose and
I have a good relationship with everyone here. We have set
up a democratic, village-style community. All decisions are
communal. Each person gets only one vote. Things have
worked out, largely, I think, because the kids are committed
to working at living.

"These kids are a new breed. Not like a lot of the kids in the
sixties who were temperamental wanderers. Those kids were
committed to having no commitment. They had no staying
power. They'd come into an established village and want to
create instantaneous change. When things didn't change,

they'd just leave. They never understood the rhythm of the land and of the people. But the people working here have a deeper understanding of time and of commitment.

"For them, like me, this place is the crystalization of a lot of vague ideas—being free, surviving in nature, living in harmony with the environment. But the kids of the sixties—and, I think, your radical changers to some extent—felt that they were nowhere. They were playing out a super–Boy Scout act —camping, surviving in the wilderness. What they didn't understand, but this new breed really accepts, is that this place is somewhere, and within it there is a balance to be found and created, that a new set of social relationships has to be developed, that new economic patterns have to be found, and an alternate society developed. You can't do any of this in six months. But I think we'll make it. We have the commitment, the energy and mutual respect to create something new. Hopefully, by next year the dream should be real."

There was a passion in Steven's eyes and voice as he talked about the future of the community. Soon afterward he was called away by a group of young men making adobe blocks. There was a bounce, a powerful jaunt in Steven's walk as he approached the building site. From a distance I watched Steven working alongside these young men with a spirit as youthful as theirs housed in the body of an old man. His sense of mission was infectious. His gentle, considered style and fiery zeal demanded commitment. I began thinking about my next trip, wondering what reality would develop from Steven's dream.

On my return, about nine months later, I saw the reality. I had stopped off at Steven's house to say hello. I found him sitting in a chair, his eyes blank with anguish and his body slack with exhaustion. He got up to greet me and then almost toppled back into the chair. He strained to lift his leg onto the hassock. His body heaved with the effort of sitting down.

He began talking, very quietly, almost to himself, at some point in mind already developed and ongoing.

"My life is filled with projects. I travel and give lectures, set up other people's ideas and make them work. My project, my dream, the one that's really important—it isn't a project, it's my life—I can't fulfill. I'm physically not up to arguing with them." Steven's voice was weakening. He stopped to recover his energy. "My body is covered with sores, and I'm always tired. The doctors can only propose a radical operation. My homeopath is stumped. He didn't even charge me for treatment. Right now, I think he's at a meeting in Greece presenting my case," Steven said with unexpected sarcasm. "I think it's psychosomatic. I can't seem to deal with this whole thing except by getting sick.

"What should I do? I started the kids on the idea of setting up a community. It's been my lifelong dream. Don't get me wrong—they're good kids and they're working hard. But they're still kids. They don't have the judgment to know what's right."

I tried to get Steven to fill me in on what had happened. He had just started when Rose came out of the kitchen, saying in angry support, "They don't listen to Steven. Everyone around the country asks Steven what to do and they listen. We offer the kids advice and they turn around and do it their own way. Like they were building a solar greenhouse and Steven set up the plans. Building takes expertise, you know. So they don't follow Steven's plans and make a mess of it. It doesn't work right and it's in such bad taste. Practically everything they build offends our sensibilities."

Steven tried to move out of his slump. "Rose, take it easy. Dave, I don't understand myself anymore. For all my idealism, I am mostly concerned about the two of us. It's our future that's at stake. That land is our security, the only money we have is invested in that land. If we go through with our original plans, that land will be tied up legally for at least five years. I'm frightened what will happen to us. It's all we have. The other thing we had was a dream for a community— I don't think it will turn out, at least not the way we planned."

Steven looked at me imploringly again, asking me "What should we do?" From the drift of his conversation, it seemed to me he knew the answer, but refused to accept it. The willfulness of the commune members, Steven's physical and psychological inability to deal with their youth and strongheadedness, his true terror of aging and need for financial security all pointed in a direction he could not accept. The dream, on Steven's terms, could never be. He couldn't have his commune and he couldn't settle for the kids' version.

He pressed me for an answer. All- I could say was "Haven't you already answered your own question?" He slumped back in the chair, a man defeated by his body and a dream that turned all too real.

Steven's tone is the gentle anger of an idealist, a man fighting to make a dream real. He sees his antagonist as an impersonal, overtechnologized, energy-destructive society. Among its legions are the Santa Fe hippies and radical career changers. Although they are perhaps well meaning, they are still dangerous. They are like the little girl who mistook the chair's texture for dirt, totally unaware of their embeddedness in a social and personal context. In their insensitivity, they see the Santa Fe landscape as "nowhere," to be colonized in their own image.

Steven, like the radical changer, sees the hippies as using the tactics and strategies of impatience. They expect the landscape to reflect their needs, their pace. They can't recognize that the life around them has its own logic, its own rhythm. Since this "nowhere" world often will not yield to their expectations—the land will not flower overnight, the local Spaniards will not reveal their consciousness immediately—the hippies leave to find a more yielding world.

But Steven doesn't see the difference between the hippies and the radical career changer as being very large. The radical career changers only have more staying power. But they are just as self-indulgent. Rather than being frustrated by life in "nowhere," they reconstitute the disastrous values of "back home," making Santa Fe resemble "somewhere." For all the radicalness of their change, they have changed only the trappings, the surface of their lives. They live in isolation, either alone or with their families, unrelated to the sources of interdependence, relying primarily on impersonal, energy-wasting services. In their seeming escape from the meaning-lessness of contemporary technological society, from the sense of alienation in work and community, the radical career changers have neither dropped out nor dropped in. They have never really left their starting point, that embeddedness in a pernicious historical present. At best they will pass through the living landscape without too much impact. At worst they will construct a new landscape that reflects the disastrous qualities of "back home."

Steven's dream is to create an alternative set of values, a demonstration of how to live meaningfully within the living landscape. It is a vision that accepts the rhythm and organization of ongoing life in which sharing and interdependence are central. It is a world that maintains an ecological and social balance, a life in which the individual lives symbiotically with the forces around him.

This dream has a seemingly selfless quality. While Steven could be accused of being self-indulgent—it is his own personal vision—he maintains its value not only for himself but for the ultimate benefit of the total environment.

However, Steven's faceless place in the dream is partly illusory. The dream's social value maintains its integrity only when Steven's needs and the dream's requirements are con-sonant. As long as Steven's personal security is not an issue, the dream can continue in anonymity. As long as the com-mune members agree to follow Steven's ideas, then the dream is paramount and selfless. But when Steven's life and the life of the community are in conflict, his idealism is pressed for an answer as to where the real commitment lies.

What has come to plague Steven is the very characteristic he separates himself from in the hippies and the radical career changers. While he criticizes them as being self-indulgent, unaware colonizers, he similarly attempts to reconstruct the life of the commune in his own image. And with disastrous effects. However moral or right Steven's views about ecology and social living, he fails to recognize that the commune members are "somewhere," a part of his living landscape. But their commitments are not his; their lives do not have his rhythm and logic. The dilemma he can't resolve is how to maintain his selfless idealism and yet be responsive to his personal needs and values.

For Steven, as for Len and other radical career changers, there is an underlying sense of wrongness, of weakness, in being self-indulgent. "Doing your thing" is for the hippie, not for the more mature, more committed individual. Yet the hippie serves an important function in the radical career changer's world, one of defining the extremity of this trait. For the radical career changer could be, and actually has been accused of being, self-indulgent. Didn't he leave his job and life back home to "do his thing" in Santa Fe? In what ways is he different, then, from the hippie?

The radical career changer can partially resolve his question of self-definition by contrast to the more extreme dropout hippie. He is a "dropin," bearing little resemblance to the kind of hippy who, as one radical career changer defined him, "comes in every summer, stoned on the *Whole Earth Catalog*, doing his number." But there is more to being a hippie than this often shared characterization suggests. These aspects are presented in the next two stories. The first is the story of Mollie, an elderly woman I met on the trip with Steven, during one of our many stops. She tells of her "hippie" life with Mike Lee and his friends. Mike's own story follows.

Overlapping Circles

Mollie's Story

After Steven turned off the main highway, we drove through what seemed like endless dry mesa country, passing a couple of trailers now and then, randomly parked, but very little else. Steven talked nostalgically about the time he first came to New Mexico. Then there was nothing out here—not even the gas stations. But New Mexico had changed, and with it, the ecological balance.

From a rutted dirt road, we pulled up at a cabin overlooking the endlessness. Its weathered adobe blended imperceptibly into the dry earth. The few plantings around the house and in the garden were fighting to maintain their color. An elderly woman came out. Her face was very finely lined. The lines softened and illuminated when she saw Rose. The two women shared a common problem. Rose had been operated on for a serious cancer, and Mollie was on the verge of a similar confrontation. They gripped each other as only two sisters could and cried.

We went into the house and sat down. Mollie offered us coffee. The house was sparsely furnished, but rich in a way that expressed its occupant. The walls were hung with her paintings and puppets. In the past few years she had given up painting and had turned to creating marionettes. With them she toured the local area, giving performances. She was now in the midst of the Christmas flurry, making cards for friends. Or at least her painter puppet was making the cards. He drew the design and signed the cards while Mollie pulled the strings. Steven and Rose persuaded Mollie to join us for lunch in a nearby town.

As we took off, Steven and I began discussing his dropping out in the 1930s. "Being a hippie isn't something new," Steven pointed out. "There were lots of people then who would be called hippies now. They lived all around me in the Everglades. But a big difference between the thirties and the sixties varieties was that we were tied up with abstract causes, really major political ideas. I remember some of my friends and I set off from Florida to California to catch a boat to China. We were going to work our way across so that we could be part of a movement called Indusco. It was a grass-roots cooperative idea that was spreading all over China. It had captured our imaginations and we wanted to be part of it. We headed off on our motorbikes with very little money.

"This was our big political vision, our great adventure. The adventure fell apart when my friend got killed on the way. But I did learn a lot about America. We had met a lot of people who had dropped out, most of them trying to find a cause."

I asked Steven if he knew Mike Lee and his hippie back-ground. I raised Mike's case to clarify Steven's contrast be-tween his time and the present hippie movement. Steven had heard about Mike but didn't know him. Then Mollie broke in from the back seat, saying that she was a good friend of Mike's. This didn't totally surprise me since even so unlikely a combination as Mollie, the sixty-year-old painter and isolate, and Mike, the vanguard hippie, was not so unusual among people in this area. I asked Mollie how she came to know Mike and she told me this story:

"I was a woman of about forty, working as an art teacher in West Virginia. I was very happy with my life until one day I got a tax form. On it, it said, 'Mollie Jones, spinster.' I had never thought of myself as a spinster, but supposedly I was since they said it on the tax form. At that point I made a decision—I wasn't going to be a spinster any longer. Not long afterwards, I met this very strange, lovely man whom I fell in love with. He was a mining engineer in New Mexico. We shared a dream. We were going to make an Eden in the desert. We found the property where the cabin is and began our life together there. I started painting for real. We planted, we farmed, and things grew in that unloving land. We led a good life.

"One day he said, on the spur of the moment, 'Let's go to Alaska. Maybe I'll get a job there or we'll just wander around.' We were poor so we needed to rent the house. This young fellow named Mike and his wife came over to look. They were passing through Santa Fe and heard about our house. They decided to take it for six months. So we packed our bags for our big holiday in the North.

"We arrived in Alaska and then three weeks later, my husband had a heart attack. I was very frightened—I had never realized how much of a child was in me. I was a strong woman before I got married—I was still a strong woman, but I didn't know what to do. I went to my husband in the hospital and cried. I felt bad because I knew he was dying. But I didn't know what to do. Where was I to go? I asked him and he said, 'Go back to the farm.' I cried and said, 'Those kids are there. I can't go back.' He said, 'Don't worry about it. Go back and everything will be all right.'

"Well, he died, and I went back, and the kids were there. Not only the two we had rented to—there were twelve others with them. They were in wigwams and tents, living all over the house in sleeping bags. It was some kind of commune. I felt very strange walking in because I didn't understand these kids.

"Mike, after listening to my story, said, 'It's no problem. We'll fix you up in a pad just like ours.' So they took my studio, put a mattress on the floor, hung a couple of mandalas on the wall. This was my pad. It was great fun; we smoked pot and I became a hippie at the age of fifty-six. We lived together that way, in real harmony, although at times I got a little disgusted with the same refried beans. I wanted something nicer to eat. But I was just as poor as they. So we sat, grumbled about the refried beans, smoked a little more pot, laughed a lot, and had a great time. I'll always remember

Mike because he gave me a whole new lease on life, and this is the lease I've been living. It's so simple—just enjoy each moment as it comes."

Overlapping Circles

Mike's Story

Silvered bus
Emptied of dreams
Filled with possibilities

No one seemed to be around. But the farm was clearly inhabited. Projects stood around in various stages of disorder. A ladder led to a roof being reshingled. Garden tools lay ready for repotting plants. A disemboweled milking machine waited to be reconstituted.

No response to my knocking. I wandered around calling "Anybody home?" No answer from the house, or the barnyard, or the flowing fields of hay shimmering in the sun.

I thought there must be somebody around. I had telephoned before coming. This was clearly the right place. Mollie had given me specific directions, and Mike had confirmed them on the phone. "Go to Las Trampas, take the left fork out of town, go past the house trailer, and take the second dirt road on the right." I was sure this was the place.

I called a few more times. No success. As I was ready to give up and drive the two hours back to Santa Fe, I saw something glistening in the field. As I approached the shine, it took the shape of a bus, vintage 1948 School. It sat in a field of green on a pedestal of wooden blocks. For all its rootednesss, the bus seemed ready for motion. It was half silver, half psychedelic, as if undecided whether to be Hippie Modern or Silver Arrow. It was being painted. Brushes and ladders were all around.

I called again. A disembodied head appeared over the top of the bus. It had a happy, smiling face and long golden hair tied in a single ponytail. On top of the head was a multi-colored knit hat, probably Mexican or Guatemalan. The head was soon joined by the body, which climbed onto the top of the bus. The well-tanned, muscled-from-hard-work body was liberally flecked with silver paint. So silver was to be the bus's color.

"I'm looking for Mike Lee. Mollie Jones told me to look him up."

"You've found him," he said, climbing down from the bus. We shook hands and sat down in the sweet-smelling grass.

"How's Mollie doing? I haven't seen her for a couple of years. She was our greatest success, maybe our only one."

"I'm not following you," I said.

"Me and my friends decided about eight years ago to leave L.A. and turn the world on. We got this bus, painted it up with really wild colors, put in a big hi-fi system, and off we went. There were four of us and our families. We headed for New Mexico because it had good vibes and it was less screwed up than most other places."

At this point, Mike launched into an abstract monologue about the city—its pollution, its inhumanity, its congestion. He had obviously thought a great deal about the problem. My interest reawakened when he returned to his own life. "We were all in show business. We thought we'd put on happenings around the country—real far-out things—lights, color, theater, music—no stops. This way people could see how much fun living was. After that we were going to buy a farm and really do the communal thing.

"We didn't get too far with it. We got to New Mexico, turned Mollie on, and a couple of other people. But we found that the communal trip was pretty heavy. I see now that we started at the wrong place. We said, 'Let's have a community and work it out from there.' We should have started as separate people, as family groups, and let whatever community was going to evolve do it by its own process. We just couldn't live together. Man needs space," Mike continued, now lauching into an abstract discussion about man's social nature.

"You know something?" Mike said. "I came to the conclusion recently that everything you do is a lesson. It teaches you something in a whole process. I used to think that the commune was a bad trip. Now I realize I had to go through it to get to this place. So there are no bad trips, just a succession of stages in the unfolding of life. And I've been through a lot of trips. Dropping out of college after three years, living down in Mexico, where I learned to use drugs. You know, I ate ninety mushrooms down there, and did I learn about dying. I had some out-of-body experiences that gave me a perspective on life. People use drugs in bad ways—to get away from self-knowledge. Me and my friends use them as ways of slicing through the bullshit of our mind. I don't use much now. I do a lot of powerful meditation."

Mike headed into a lecture comparing drugs and meditation as consciousness raisers. His analysis was interrupted by the sound of a car bumping along the road.

"That must be my old lady and the kids," Mike said. "Let's go over to the house. We'll have some lunch and talk some more."

We started off.

The sun was warm as we pushed a path through the field of high grass. The bruised stalks flowered into a perfume that spoke of sun and sky and land. As we neared the house, these smells of life were echoed, in human terms, by the sounds of Mike's two children. They were chasing each other, in and out of a huge Japanese bathtub. They were trying very hard not to catch each other. The fun was in the running and screaming.

As we entered the house, Mike's wife was setting out lunch. Her excitement was unbounded. She could hardly get the words out fast enough. "The Maharishi was fantastic. Everyone was really turned on. Vegas did a solo 'being' thing like you'd done with him on the farm. Everything was good, the vibes were high. The mountains were really pretty with all the wild flowers." She went on for a while mentioning names and places that were totally unfamiliar to me.

Mike broke the rush of words by introducing me. He tried to fill me in on what his wife was talking about. "Maharishi had a two-day thing up in the mountains. I turned on to him a couple of years ago before he became 'big-time.' The meditation he taught me was really strong. It gave me a distance from my life so I could see what it was all about. I got that distance with drugs but in a different way. After working with him, I decided to give up the show business and get back to myself."

"Wait, you skipped a couple of things," I said in dismay. "You left me in Mexico with the out-of-body experience. Fill me in from there."

"OK, sure. I grew up in L.A. and my family has always been involved, in some way, in movies. I came back from Mexico and was offered a job as road manager with a big-name band. I worked with them for three years and then I started working for a big-deal director as his personal assistant. I had a good time, enjoyed the work, and had a lot of glamour and money and everything else. But then I got into the meditation and saw it was time to move along in the process of my life. It was weird, after I started meditating, I thought to myself—I was in a health club at the moment, working out—what I thought was, life was really screwed up if you have to pay money and make a job of keeping your body in shape. Out here, it just comes natural. Your break your ass fixing and farming, and for no cost at all you get a good body." Mike flexed his muscles. Everything rippled, as in a Charles Atlas ad. The kids, who had just come in, thought this was great. They kept asking their father to ripple different muscles, like a contortionist or maybe like a belly dancer. Mike's face was aglow with smiles.

"So I pulled out of the movies and came out with the commune. Vegas is one of my closest friends from the commune. He's one of the only ones left around. He and I used to do this 'being' thing—trying to get people to be aware of themselves and what's around them. No drugs, just singing, exercises, running, and jumping. People were very into themselves when they started, but they were relating and enjoying it pretty quickly."

Neither of us had noticed that the family had left. We walked out on the porch to see where they had gone. We saw them over in the barnyard milking the goats. Watching their activity, I asked Mike whether the farm was going to be the end of 'trips.'

"No way. Life is always in process. That I learned out here. I thought, when I started farming three years ago, that I'd found my place. I dig farming. I make enough to live. The farm feeds us. For extra bread I paint houses sometimes, sell plants sometimes, collect food stamps sometimes. Most everything is cool, but for one thing—this place possesses me. I have to work constantly to keep it going. And I don't get enough time to be with my wife and kids. And that's what I want to do now. I've watched the process of the farm and us in it. Now I want to understand the process of just us, like watching the kids grow, and me grow with them.

"The farm won't let me be. What I've learned is very simple—more is sometimes less. So we're cutting down our lives and moving into the bus. I'll paint over the psychedelic— that was from another time, a different me. I'll fix up the inside and make it livable. It should take a month to get it ready. Then we hit the road. The thing is to be together. We can manage the bread. You really don't need much to live on. I learned that here too."

We talked for a long time. The light subtly changed on the snow-capped mountain peaks, drawing out deeper and deeper shadows. As I was leaving, Mike pointed in the direction of the bus. "That's really strange. The grass hasn't bent back to cover over the path we made. It should have. It's been a couple of hours. Maybe it's a sign that getting the bus ready is the right thing. It's always nice to have a sign. I don't need it, though. I am totally convinced that this is the right move for the next stage in the process."

Mike and Steven have the same adversary, an overtechnologized, dehumanizing society. But the antagonist has a different quality, a different definitional shape for each. Steven's enemy has clear features, an oppressing tangibility. Mike's foe is more abstract, amorphous, residing in the vague form of "society."

Perhaps these different ways of specifying the enemy arise from their respective sensibilities and clarity of understanding. Yet there is an important relation between their attitudes toward social change and how well defined the enemy is. As Steven correctly diagnosed, the thirties generation believed in social ideologies, in abstract causes. Embodied in these dreams was the strong hope and belief that the bases of dehuminization and environmental destruction could be meaningfully changed. And change would occur through concerted social action, under the banner of a cause. Change was a real possibility that required the problems to be specifically defined so that they could be remedied.

For Mike's generation, the hippies of the sixties, specific definition is not needed. There is a disillusionment with change, at least on an abstract level of social causes. If there is any solution, any possible basis for a shared dream, it is on a personal level. Mike and his commune members are committed to the dream of "turning people on," a projection of their personal joy in living. By implication the "turn-on" suggested that social change will not occur by traditional methods and values, by believing that the tide can be modified by social action. In fact, they view such beliefs as creating a blindness to the very essence of living, namely, that it is a process involving joy and experiencing for the goal of self-growth. If change is to occur, it will be through a subversion of society, through a revolution in consciousness.

It was this personal "turn-on" that gave Mollie a new lease on life. After her husband's death and the end of their shared hopes, Mike's vision provided a new meaning for her life. It had only marginally to do with pot smoking, mandalas, and communal living. These were more stage settings, punctuation points, for the message of grasping the moment, experiencing the nature of humanness, being happy in living.

In a sense, the hippie's dream is a more destructive indictment of society than Steven's or the radical career changer's. By both implication and example it says that all social forms, whether manners, action, or commitment, are illusory in providing meaning. They bypass, and provide a poor substitute for, the essential personal value of self-growth. Unless you "do your own thing" there is little meaning to doing somebody else's.

Yet for all the actual or covert criticisms suggested by Mike's life style, his ongoing activities are not greatly different from those he criticizes. He too is responsible to his family; he too must earn a livelihood for them to survive. But there is one important difference. He does not vest any of his activities with ultimate meaning and value. Each activity has intrinsic meaning and requires commitment. But in a broader perspective, these meanings are valid primarily as lessons for the next stage of activity. If they intrude on the essential core of his life, on his enjoyment of self and others, like the farm possessing him, the commitments are given up. Commitments for Mike are serviceable and negotiable, not ultimately meaningful.

Here lies an essential difference between the hippie and the radical career changer. While both share in the same activities of living—family, work, social relations—they invest their activities with different levels of commitment and permanence. The radical career changer, more than the hippie, believes in the validity of goals, the final outcomes of activity. He sinks his roots deeper by creating a permanent home, committing himself to accomplishing a good job even in a work setting that may be demeaning. Against these values, which differ little from "back home," he sees the hippie as transient and uncommitted. In the work setting, an area where the radical career changer is often competitive with the hippie, the hippie is seen as doing shoddy work because of a lack of investment. The former social service administrator turned welfare recipient and jack-of-all-trades put it this way: "I found a lot of kids who had never really worked to make a living. It really gets me mad. The one thing that I learned, that's always been a part of me, is to do a good job. These kids would come in, learn the craft, do a slipshod job, and then whoever was in charge or had to vouch for them would be left holding the bag. I got burned too many times. I really wonder about those kids and what they are doing. They just come in telling how committed they are to all sorts of ideals and then disappear. They have a very short attention span, especially when it comes to work. There are some who have stayed and have really done a good job, but on the whole they're a bad lot. I hate to sound as conservative as the people in Oklahoma, but I've lived too long with a lot of bullshit and no output."

While this criticism is perhaps well taken, or more appropriate to the excesses in some hippies' views, their retort might be "Don't vest meaning in the stage settings of life, like work. Meaning lies in self-growth, and work has value, is only worth involvement, when it has a personal 'turn-on.' "

In this sense the hippie is more self-indulgent than the radical career changer in making himself the center of meaning. Yet, from another angle, the radical career changer's solution to his life situation is far more personal, particularly in relation to his role in society. In encountering Steven's and Mike's antagonists—the dehumanization of work, the oppressive ecological and social environments—the radical career changer chose to solve these broad problems in a very individual way. The problems were defined as specific to an actual work or environmental setting. The solution was seen in personal terms of finding a new work setting and a new environment. He neither attacks nor subverts his opponents. He attempts an escape, a defection from encounter. Yet the escape may be hollow, as Steven suggests. Without a broad social consciousness and awareness, the radical career changer runs the risk of reconstructing "back home" in Santa Fe. Moreover, his solution adds little to social or moral change.

Then, which is the better solution—Steven's idealism, Mike's self-oriented answer, or the radical career changer's more personal salvation? Is the better answer, if there is one, necessarily the right and moral solution? Against what measure can an individual gauge the adequacy of his solution?

These questions pose not only difficult philosophical problems but also deeply personal dilemmas. The stories in the next chapter illuminate some important facets of these questions, particularly in relation to decisions about settling in Santa Fe.

THE COSTS OF CHANGING

Santa Fe, like any environment, is naturally selective. It draws some people. It repels others. Some who come are maintained —they are able to survive. Others find the environment inhospitable. They move on, seeking a more supportive setting, some place where they can settle and find a niche.

Many people find Santa Fe so alluring that they talk of relocating there. But this is mostly idle fantasy, a way of underlining their enjoyment. For all of the enticements of living in Santa Fe, they will return happily to their home. While it may lack many of Santa Fe's virtues, it is still home. It is a place where they can earn a livelihood; it is a world where they can find meaning and purpose for their lives; it is a setting where they have social embeddedness within the acceptable sameness of predictability. And home has the sense of rootedness, a feeling often so powerful that people will accept the imminence of natural or economic catastrophe to live there. The hold of "home" can be so strong that dislocation is perceived as a punishment not unlike exile. For those who go back home, the potential move to Santa Fe becomes a gentle dream to be invoked when life at home becomes problematic.

For others, the move to Santa Fe is a more real possibility. For them, "back home" does not have the same compelling power. Because of dissatisfaction with work, social relations, sameness, or whatever, these people will explore more realistically the option of relocating in Santa Fe. In evaluating this possibility, they soon will learn that surviving in Santa Fe is difficult. Jobs are almost as scarce as water. Santa Fe's two major industries, tourism and home construction, seldom go wanting for willing, underpaid employees. Establishing a professional practice is likely not to be any more successful. To provide a clientele for all the many varieties of mental health practitioners in Santa Fe would require disturbance of epidemic proportions. There are admittedly some state government jobs. But these usually go to long-term residents. The would-be settler is thus faced with the eventuality of having to maintain a holding pattern, sustaining himself until welfare becomes effective or until he can ferret out one of the few jobs, or until his self-created employment finds a clientele.

Knowing the harsh economic realities, the potential Santa Fe emigré must decide whether the risks of relocation are too high. But to calculate only on the basis of economic cost would be foolhardy. There are also psychological risks that must be considered in making the decision. They involve how the individual will adjust to a likely shift in role definition, lowered income and status, and a possible redefinition of his life's direction. There is also the possible adjustment to learning that many of Santa Fe's enticing features could easily turn into problems. The appealing slow pace of Santa Fe's life can prove to be a source of distress for a determined person seeking to accomplish things, whether in his work or social life. Or the many pleasant social relations can turn into hollow interactions when the focus of the relationship is consistently turned inward, toward self-growth, rather than upon an external reality. Or even the nonjudgmental, accepting attitude of Santa Fe residents may be a cloak for not caring and complacency. But these potential psychological adjustments are difficult to assess from a vantage point outside Santa Fe. They must be experienced in the setting itself.

The radical career changer has paid many of these costs, both psychological and economic, for the opportunity to live in Santa Fe. Given that he has remained in Santa Fe (of those I interviewed the range of residency was from two to twenty-six years, with a mode of six years), the price was apparently not too high. He has managed to survive. He has found a place for himself. He projects his future as being set in Santa Fe.

However, inferring the costs of being in Santa Fe from the

lives of the radical career changers provides a partial, biased estimate. They are the satisfied consumers. Would the price tag necessarily look the same for the less satisfied consumers, those who never came or those who have left?

For every person who stays in Santa Fe, there are many more who either choose not to come or decide (or are forced) to leave. There are those ambivalent friends of the radical career changer who would like to make the move yet think it would be crazy. There are the Santa Fe commuters who periodically come to visit, trying to check out the possibilities. There are those who come, find the possibilities too few, and leave. They know they cannot survive the harsh economic realities. There are also those who settle, who do survive, but find the costs of remaining in Santa Fe too high and leave.

All these absent people are very much part of the story of the radical career changer in this special environment. Their stories illuminate the factors leading to the choice of relocating and staying in Santa Fe, and the costs involved in these decisions.

Here, then, are the stories of four such absent people. Although none presently lives in Santa Fe, each has either seriously considered or tried living there.

Never-Never Land

David's Story

The air was still hot and close when I arrived at the school. It was six-thirty. Registration for our "innovation in learning," our college without walls and structure, was about to begin. We had advertised, printed brochures, talked with people. Everybody said, "Great idea," "Exciting program," "Just what Santa Fe needs."

Seven o'clock—no students. Perhaps people were still eating dinner.

I realized that I had fallen into the Santa Fe trap. Only one foot, mind you. Even social scientists are not immunized against their subject matter. I was in love with Santa Fe. Maybe not the town so much, but the landscape and the people. Not the Spanish and Indian segments—they were not readily accessible. They seemed to exist mostly in the Anglos' stories. My people were the "losers and seekers," as one of the local clergymen called them. I shared with them that pervasive problem of how to make a living so I could settle in Santa Fe. One of the losers, who was a winner economically, told me, "If everyone who wanted to come here could survive, this place would be ten times as big." I learned quickly that if you want to survive you have to create your own employment. Or you're left with the few seasonal jobs serving the tourist trade. Or you could farm. But the soil is harder—dry, unresponsive, uncaring about your survival.

So you find a need and create a service and pray that someone will really want it. So I created a college. Others created an occult book shop, or a health food store, or a new form of therapy. Some stay, most go. One of the longer-term transients complained, "It's hard to establish relationships. People come and go. They're mostly here about a year. They can't make the bread. So they go away and come back with enough. And they leave when the bread runs out."

Seven-thirty. Air is cooling down. My God, there are three cars coming up the road. Students! Why are they passing the entrance and parking down the road? First to emerge from each car is a dog. Soon the air is filled with commands: Stop! Heel! Fetch! I thought fleetingly of instantaneously creating a course in "The Metaphysics of Dogdom" and recruiting the dog trainers or perhaps even the dogs. They were the nearest thing to students I had seen.

Eight-fifteen. There is a rising chill. It is getting dark. People couldn't still be eating dinner.

Another car drove up the road. I didn't pay much attention. Probably another dog trainer. Looking around, I saw that the dogs had left. So had their trainers. The car pulled right up in front of me. I grabbed my registration forms. A bearded young man got out, smiled at me, and walked past to one of the classrooms. I called eagerly, asking whether he was looking for me and the school. He responded quietly, "No, I'm here for a transcendental meditation class." He disappeared into the room. Was he the teacher or the student, or maybe both?

A few minutes later, another car pulled up. From this one emerged an ascetic, straight-looking guy in a business suit with a tie. Something you never see in Santa Fe. He even carried an attaché case. I didn't ask whether he was looking for me. I simply said, "You must belong to the transcendental meditation class."

"I'm the teacher," he said. "I drive in every night from Los Alamos to teach. Excuse me. My student is waiting."

He drove thirty miles to teach one student? And here I had the delusion of humanity beating down our nonwalls. Maybe he had acquired his ascetic look trying to live off the income of one student. Or maybe transcendental meditation changes one's survival needs. I'd have to check that one out.

Things were very quiet. The sun had almost set, filling the sky with a crimson glow over the mountains. Black masses outlined against red. Beneath them, the twinkle of Santa Fe's lights. They seemed irrelevant, or perhaps inappropriate, in this powerful landscape. From this angle, Santa Fe looked like never-never land.

Perhaps it's the power of this setting that defines the tempo and attitude of many of the people who come here. A friend put it this way. "When you have to wait ten minutes till the water comes into the irrigation ditch and there is no way to make it come in nine minutes or eight minutes, then you relax and watch it run. So it's easy not to hassle things." *Mañana*, tomorrow, will do. Another sense of never-never land. Probably the real draw for the losers and seekers. Relationships become easy because nothing really has to get done. People can be open. They have the time to explore themselves, their needs and consciousness. All the services that are created to survive aren't really necessary for anyone else's survival. So why rush?

I couldn't come to terms with *mañana*. The tempo made me feel good, really at home. My friends always seemed to have the time to be friends. Nothing was ever so pressing that we couldn't grab the moment, maybe tripping off the mountains, or just sitting around, or just being free to be free.

But would the pace get to me in the long run? Could I live without any real involvement? Somehow, "doing my thing," whatever that happened to be, was too loose a structure. I wasn't comfortable with it. Would my dream of being completely open to possibility turn into a nightmare if I finally got hold of it? Maybe the dream was a good crutch. It propped up a life that couldn't really be lived without boundaries. I somehow needed the embeddedness of my life's tensions. *Mañana* might be too pleasant, too soft. I might lose that edge, mellow out. Then the movement of my life would step down, crawl toward pleasantness. I had seen this happen often in Santa Fe, although I didn't want to see it at first. Despite that danger, might I really be able to live here permanently? No more commuting. How tempting. But would *mañana* get me?

Those who can't adjust to this rhythm are those who leave. They can't survive. They can't grasp the moment, and a livelihood as it comes, if it comes. Many wait, existing for *mañana*. They are the ones who consume all those services that allow others to survive.

Like my friend Kathy. She had stopped at my house briefly to tell me about an acupuncture course she was taking, then had excused herself for the rushed visit. "I've got to go home and check my mail. See you later." She was waiting for a letter about an admission interview for graduate training. The moment hadn't arrived. She had been waiting for six weeks. She must be used to waiting. After divorcing her husband, she had come to Santa Fe, mostly by accident. With the little money from her part-time job as a secretary and some money from the men she occasionally lived with, she had enough income and time to try many of Santa Fe's survival services. Rolfing, Gudjieff, macrobiotic cooking—among others—had passed through her life as the teachers and gurus had passed through Santa Fe. She waits for the letter. She waits for an answer.

I wonder whether the letter will come. Most likely it will and she'll go. But she probably won't make it. Her life, her work, her feelings are ridden through with ennui, that lack of engagement from waiting too long. That waiting, that yearning for something or someone to provide a meaning. So she waits for that eternal letter. *Mañana.*

Nine-thirty. It's dark now. The air is cold. My waiting is over for tonight. I get into the car. Another round tomorrow night. The transcendental meditation class, all two of them, closes down. The classroom light goes out. All is quiet. Will tomorrow be different?

After three such nights the local newspaper announced "New College Intellectual Success, Financial Disaster." Thus my decision not to relocate in Santa Fe was, in part, made for me. The difficult economics of surviving clearly said "Don't come." At least not on your terms.

My terms were to create my own employment and not accept Santa Fe's usual survival solution of being a waiter or a construction worker. Although such work was not beneath my dignity, I saw it as meaningless and unfulfilling. And its emptiness couldn't be filled by all of Santa Fe's wonderful features. Neither the landscape, nor friends, nor freedom could make palatable the idea that work's only meaning and purpose would become simply survival. Work would become toil, justified only by the enjoyment of the few remaining off hours. I could not accept this idea. It denied my belief that work must have meaning and purpose beyond receiving a paycheck. Without meaningful work, living lacked purpose. To distinguish between work and leisure, to trade one off for the other, was naive. It uncritically assumed that living can be separated into impermeable, noninteracting compartments. If in order to live in Santa Fe I had to work in such a meaningless way, then the price was far too high. I was unwilling to pay for it. The cost was too dear for a way of life that demanded from me a fundamental redefinition of my sense of living.

To live anywhere, whether back home or in Santa Fe, I needed a purpose, a feeling of mission. This the college provided. Its existence fulfilled my long-held dream of creating a meaningful, productive educational setting. It would serve not only my need to survive but also the educational needs of the community. I saw it as having more value than the consumerism of many of Santa Fe's self-created employment situations.

What I attempted to develop was an educational environment, a setting for intellectual scholarship and learning based on a mutuality of interests. It was to be a contractual world in both economic and educational terms. The staff would define their interests; those people who found these concerns congenial would, I hoped, enroll. The students and staff, if that distinction could be meaningfully maintained, would then negotiate whatever fees were needed, their shared educational directions and goals, the location and scheduling of meetings, and so on. There would be no need for buildings, large administrative staffs, or other complex, expensive institutional machinery—the interpersonal, educational interaction did not require such staging. The college, as an institution, had little other function than to maintain the intellectual values of the staff's offerings and to make the educational encounter possible through coordinating the search for interested participants.

The economic failure of the college largely resided in the potential students' *mañana* attitude. Many of the people who had voiced strong interest in our offerings never enrolled.

Later they said, in effect, "You know, this is Santa Fe. *Mañana* will always do. I'm sorry, but I just never got around to signing up. When does the next semester begin?" There was no next semester, since I soon learned that economic survival often required at least three years of back-up funding to outlive the *mañana* perspective. I didn't have that kind of money. Nor was the staff willing to invest their own capital in the school's survival. While they seemingly accepted the idea of a college as a scholar's cooperative, they preferred to forgo any real commitment to creating their own school. Strangely enough, here was a group of highly trained, well-established academics and professionals, many of whom had rejected standard institutional thinking back home, now falling back into traditional expectations and forms. I was unwilling to compromise or negotiate on the issue of shared commitment and responsibility for the college. Thus the school as an approach to learning could not survive.

I tried to pass off my unsuccessful attempt at fulfilling my dream by saying "At least the loss is tax deductible" or "For a paltry six hundred dollars I played out a dream and became an instant celebrity too." Accepting the failure was made easier by understanding that the staff and potential students both shared in the negative aspect of Santa Fe's *mañana* perspective—an unwillingness to risk commitment. In a world where nothing had to get accomplished, the students perceived the college's intellectual venture as an entertaining distraction that, like many other of Santa Fe's possibilities, could wait till *mañana*. For the staff, Santa Fe's normative *mañana* attitude sustained the view that by committing their energy and resources to the school they would be restricting their freedom.

Admittedly, Santa Fe's slower pace offered an ease in living. This I valued highly. But the university's demise clearly defined my already growing sense of *mañana*'s darker side. Under its spell, I recognized in myself and others a weakening of purpose, a decline in passion to accomplish, an unwillingess to make firm commitments. My brief encounter with Kathy only served to underline the ennui that could easily take hold in the never-never land of Santa Fe. I realized how easy it was to become cut off from the outside world. Being embedded in the comfort of not having to accomplish too much and without the tension inherent in striving, I could project myself as entering into a supportive womb that would eventually smother me. *Mañana* seemed antithetical to tension, that state of discomfort necessary for me to maintain a sense of purpose and development in my life.

Looking back, I believe that had the college thrived, I still would not have come to Santa Fe. The decision would have been made immensely more difficult by the college's success, but it would have been the same. By the time of registration, my unbridled enthusiasm for living in Santa Fe had been tempered; I was torn between my love for Santa Fe and my fears about what a move might mean.

My ambivalence about relocating was finally resolved by an event that happened soon after the failure of the school. One of my closest friends and role model for being a "free spirit" gleefully told me that he had found a job. During his first two years in Santa Fe he was mostly unemployed. He seemed happy with traveling around, farming, picking up odd jobs, and working at keeping his options open. Now, even with his apprehensions about losing his freedom and the constraints of structured work, he was looking forward to the straight, unfree life of an administrator. All his fears and concerns seemed little more than feeble asides to maintain his former self-image. My model for grasping the moment, of being free, had grown clay feet. I wondered whether my other "free" friends would similarly turn coat if they could find a reasonable job. One thing I knew for sure. My friend and I were sufficiently similar that I could sensibly project what my hoped-for unstructured life would look like if it became more permanent. I then started to question whether the unstructured life really had as much value as I had originally believed. Was it a goal that

I should strive toward, or was it only a substitute for a lack of meaning and purpose in living? Although I haven't yet answered this question, my friend's positive transformation in leaving the unstructured life for the world of work informed me that the cost of freedom would be too high for me to pay.

Having decided that the economic and psychological prices of relocating in Santa Fe were far more expensive than those involved in remaining back home, I was faced with a double-edged problem: how to create or find the positive values I had experienced in Santa Fe and how to reduce the cost of living in a faster-paced world, where structure was too often confining and meaningless and where social relations were usually defined by social prescriptions rather than by the nature of the relationship itself. This problem still engages me.

Similar concerns are revealed in the next story. Here Greg evaluates the possibility of giving up his job as a vice-president of a large corporation to be an artist in Santa Fe. While "back home" has many sources of frustration, he is happy with it. Yet he feels he would be happier and more satisfied in Santa Fe. His cost accounting of options is a model of dispassionate analysis. Yet it is subtly suffused with a passionate moral sense. While he has assuaged his moral concerns and his book-keeping indicates that a move to Santa Fe is financially feasible, it seems unlikely that he will make a radical change. He will likely remain one of those absent Santa Fe people, perhaps a sometime commuter, who will invoke radical career change as an option when work and life back home are not satisfying.

Color Coding

Greg's Story

"May I have your name, please?"
"David Krantz."
The young woman behind the desk turned to a small

switchboard that looked like a crazy quilt of colored buttons. After a very brief, inaudible conversation, she returned and officiously said, "Mr. Faber will see you. His office is 907. You can take a red elevator on your right."

As I started past her, from the cold, white marble of the entrance foyer to the seemingly warmer space toward the elevator, she continued, sounding like a prerecorded tape, "You'll have to wear this identifying badge."

She gave me a plastic badge with the word VISITOR printed in large block letters. Pinning it on my jacket, I approached the red elevators. They were indeed red, you couldn't miss that. The carpet was red, having changed in midfloor from gray. I looked behind me to find gray elevators. In front of me was a wall totally red, as were the closed elevator doors. The elevator soon arrived. A crowd of animated people got off. It was quitting time. I entered to find, not to my surprise, that the interior was red.

When I arrived at the ninth floor, having been entertained by barely audible nonmusic, Greg was waiting. He greeted me and then started showing me around. We entered an enormous open space filled with desks. The area was artfully broken up, with malice of design aforethought, by low partitions, an apparent random spacing of desks, and the omnipresent color coding. Green areas, leading to beige sections, flowing into a wide gray-blue stripe apparently pointing to a corridor done in autumnal rust. "I assume that the really important things happen down that corridor?" I asked.

"Of course." Greg smiled. "You notice we not only change the color but also the texture. Much thicker, more opulent. The corridor is where the executive offices for the division are. Each one has real floor-to-ceiling walls, a view of the bridge, and the officer's personal choice of color."

As we entered Greg's office, soft in muted blues, I asked, "Could you have chosen puce, or pitch black, to express yourself?"

"Well, there is only so much you can get away with when you are vice-president. The secret of running a good business is total freedom within an unseen autocracy. Take off your jacket and relax. Our wives won't be here for another hour or so."

Loosening his tie, Greg went over to a bar disguised as an office console. "It still gives me a kick when I think how the four of us have hit it off, all of it starting with a mutual friend back in Milwaukee. And remember your shock, that first night we met, when you were telling me about your work in Santa Fe and I said that I hoped to be there in five years if not sooner? Is Scotch all right?"

I nodded. "I remember. But I'm still not convinced that you'll give up all this—well, OK, maybe you can give up the color coding—but not the position and the kind of money you're making, to be an artist in Santa Fe."

"But I am serious," Greg said with emphasis. "Sure, I like all the comforts that income and status bring. There's no question of that. But I think the price tag is getting too high. When I have enough money to ensure that Nancy and the kids are taken care of—the kids will be able to go to college and Nancy has some security—then we'll do it."

"I guess what I am having trouble with is that on the one hand you told me you like your job and your life style. It's obvious from your office and title that in the ten years you've been in the business world you've been very successful. Am I right so far?"

Greg nodded, sitting meditatively in his chair.

"Yet you'd give up this to scratch out a life as an artist?"

"Dave, I may be a dewy-eyed romantic, but not when it comes to my life and my family. I've thought a lot about the move, and I've checked out many of the angles. To put it simply, I'm going to Santa Fe because I'm tired of this war that is euphemistically called corporate life. Like, take the color coding. You picked up on it, but most people who oversee it or work in it don't have a glimmer of what it's about. Working is like the old good-news-and-bad-news joke. Do you know it?"

Noting my incomprehension, he continued, "The beater comes into the hold of one of those Roman galleys. He tells the slaves to stop rowing. That's good news already. He announces that he has some good news and some bad news. 'But first,' he says, 'the good news: tonight everyone gets double rations of bread and water.' Shouts and cheers. 'And more good news: double rations of rum.' Sheer pandemonium. He whips them into silence. 'And now for the bad news.' " Greg stopped momentarily, relishing the punch line. " 'The bad news is that the captain is going water skiing tomorrow.' "

"What you're saying is that you can make work conditions pleasant but it doesn't change the work itself."

"My job has two descriptions—one is the corporation's, the other is mine. When I entered corporate life, I was hired with no business training. I had been doing social work before, working with street gangs in Baltimore. Business is enlightened in trying to make the employees happy. So they hired me to deal with the workers. But corporations are big, and for all their benevolence, they still can be very shortsighted and often immoral. When economics get bad, people get fired. It becomes a pissing match, starting from the top down. One part of my job is to make the life of the fired person somehow more pleasant, cool him out with warmth, love, and good-natured help. But from the corporate point of view the important thing is that he is fired. I don't question the desire for more humane treatment—that's good. But the corporation doesn't examine the bases for the firing or its impact on the person's life. Those questions are simply answered in cost-accounting terms. That's their definition, not mine. I've been a maverick and have questioned a lot of what's going on here. To have gotten away with it and even made it work for me has been my good luck. But it's a constant war, and I'm tired of fighting it."

"Then why did you get into it at all? You must have had some idea about what it would be like."

"Sure, I did. But it couldn't be any worse than social work.

At least corporate life wouldn't have as much of the do-good, pseudomorality bullshit of those people. When social workers started calling themselves professionals—which meant that they were ten notches better than their clients and could now tell those unfortunate poor what was good for them—I knew that social work wasn't a life for me. I understood the gangs I worked with because I had grown up on the streets. But my mode of operation was unorthodox. Clearly not professional."

"It sounds like social work was war, too."

"Most things are. You just have to learn the rules or you don't survive. I vaguely understood this while I was growing up. When I left the streets to go to college, I had more of a glimmer. Then the rules changed again when I went into the army. I had an experience in the service that made the point extremely clear. I was in bayonette practice, doing a good job of stabbing the dummies. Everyone around me was screaming 'Kill!' That was the segeant's instruction—get into it, see the dummies as 'gooks,' get angry, kill them. I couldn't get into that, so I went along doing my job, just bayonetting in silence. The sergeant came over and chewed me out for not saying 'Kill.' I told him I didn't believe in killing but that I'd do it if I had to. I explained that I couldn't accept the whole attitude of the exercise. I was then sent to the commanding officer. He said, 'Faber, I see by your record that you have some college. But you're in the army now. And you even volunteered. So what's this all about?' I explained again. He tried to reason with me. To no avail. Finally, he said in a fatherly tone, 'Faber, you can do bayonette practice without saying "Kill" and you can do it as long as you want, through all your repetitions of basic training. Am I making myself clear?' It was all too clear. So I went back, did some more bayonetting, and said 'Kill.' Not very loud, mind you."

"I sense that you have some rules for your own life, but I can't put them together, especially with your plans to go to Santa Fe."

"You're sounding like a psychologist. What do you see as my rules?"

"Well, I see a strong moral commitment, a need to make a contribution. I also sense a Machiavellian quality to your work life. You want to get somewhere both in the corporation and in terms of your life style. For all your frustrations, you seem to like your work. Putting them all together, why go to Santa Fe?"

"I'm not sure that all the facets have to fit. Sure, I like my work. I'm almost a borderline workaholic. I like the challenge of finding my way, of understanding how corporate life works. That's part of why I left my previous corporate job. I saw all these guys standing in line waiting to go nowhere. And they were starting to mistake getting a better paycheck as getting somewhere. I wanted to get to the top, to see how it worked. My former boss said that I had made fantastic progress for a guy of thirty-eight. 'Wait, it'll all come,' he said. So I went shopping for a job where I could be in on the top level of decision making, talk one-on-one with senior people. The reason for that was not only the challenge of the work. It was also because I think I am right in what I believe and I wanted to prove it. That's why I came on board here two years ago. It wasn't only making it in terms of position and income, but also so that I could accomplish more in making people's work lives more livable, more human."

"And you are frustrated because you can't accomplish that."

"I've done better here because I've had more power. But the structure of business is set up to be not very supportive to these ideas. And higher-level decision making is just as much of a pissing match as the lower-level stuff."

"Instead of going to Santa Fe, why not compromise? Keep working, trying to help, but invest some of your energies in other things."

"No way. I can't do that kind of juggling. I can't separate my life into work and nonwork. I'd be like those guys waiting to go nowhere and not caring about work except as a larger paycheck. All the things they buy, all the trips they take, all the hobbies they get passionate about are really poor substitutes for the satisfaction of doing a good, committed job. I can't live with that compromise. Either I'll make my peace with corporate life, at least partially on my terms, or I'm giving it up for Santa Fe."

"But wouldn't you be copping out on your moral responsibilities by going to Santa Fe?"

"Maybe. I feel that I've paid my moral dues. I believe that each of us owes something to society for being alive. I think I've paid my debt. Now it's time to rest; it's time for me. I want a slower pace. I look forward to a relaxed dinner, looking out at that beautiful landscape, spending more time with my family, doing my art work. I was pretty good as a painter, but that was a long time ago. Let me turn the psychological tables for a minute. I wonder why you seem to be having more trouble with the Santa Fe idea than me?"

Greg's comment stopped me. It started me thinking. He said, after a short time, "I wonder whether it has to do with your 'crisis' notion. All the people you have written about were in some state of crisis before coming to Santa Fe, and, for them, it was probably a way of resolving their problems. If that's the model you're working from, it doesn't fit me. I hope I have enough foresight to plan my life sensibly in terms of what my family and I need rather than letting it reach crisis proportions."

"Perhaps you're right." I was still working out an idea, trying to verbalize an ill-defined notion. "Let me think out loud and see if it makes any sense. Wouldn't your choice be really an early retirement? There are a lot of people in Santa Fe who have enough money to live comfortably without a need to work. They didn't come out in crisis or take much risk in making the move."

"It seems to me," Greg said, in a considered, thoughtful way, "the issue is not the category I fit in. The real question for the radical career changer or the early-retirement person, and for me—and that's another element I haven't solved—is how much will the move support or take away from what's really important to me and my family. I won't be that financially flush to give up work altogether. I think I can tolerate the lower income from being an artist. And the status change from vice-president to artist doesn't hang me up. But there really are two questions I have to answer before I make the move: can I establish enough security before going and is the move the right one for my needs at this stage of life?"

"What does Nancy think about this?"

"She's unsure. She's trying, as you know, to start a career. She hasn't invested the career bit with as much romance as most women returning to work, but I think she still sees it as a way to a kind of fulfillment. She has a right to find out what I've learned about work." Greg smiled knowingly at me. "And Nancy's needs are another consideration to take into account in making the move."

The buzzer on the intercom sounded. Greg answered, "Tell them we'll be right down." He turned to me and said, "Nancy and your lovely wife are downstairs. Rather than expose them to the color coding, let's go down and meet them."

We left his office, walking past the color-coded general office space. We stopped in front of the gray elevator.

"How come we're not taking the red ones?" I asked.

"The red ones are for those people who really don't know the rules of the game. The gray ones are for the ones who don't like standing in line waiting to go nowhere." Noting my bewilderment, Greg commented, "It's an in-house joke. Most executives use gray because they go between the top, at nine, and the lobby, without much need to stop along the way. Are you sure you want to know the hidden mysteries of color coding?"

For all the cold precision of Greg's cost accounting, there is a powerful sense of morality which informs and defines his analysis. This morality pervades his work life. It is so central that he will not compromise it—either he maintains a total commitment or leaves that world of work. Similarly, his responsibility to family is primary and nonnegotiable. Believing that he has paid his moral dues to society, he can consider withdrawing from confrontation. Everything else—income, status, and power—is negotiable. By defining his priorities, Greg has made his present and future options more intelligible. His morality becomes the cutting edge to pare down his possibilities.

Staying in corporate life is not a plausible choice. His work, while exciting, demanding, fulfilling, and rewarding, is seen as ultimately futile. Although work's value as a way of accomplishing a moral good is still partially intact, its meaning is viewed as somewhat illusory and ultimately short-lived. He knows he can accomplish his purpose only with the permission of corporate life. And this permission becomes harder to obtain as his power and threat value increase. He may be given permission to change particular colors, but never to attack the idea of color coding. To compromise and remain in corporate life would mean falling into the abhorred purgatory of "waiting in line to go nowhere, believing that the paycheck defines the meaning of work and living." A meaningless life that could ultimately lead to crisis. Nor is the option of taking another job likely to improve his situation. The immorality Greg perceives is not specific to his job or his corporation. It is inherent in all situations, whether business or social work, where power is inequitable and the structure is inflexible, unyielding.

Nor can Greg accept the possibility of juggling, of trading off work for leisure. These two aspects of life are inseparable for him. The only acceptable option that seemingly remains is to give up his present life and move to Santa Fe.

Santa Fe represents the end of fighting. It is a place where there are no wars, or if they do exist, they will be fought at a slower pace. The *mañana* tempo is valued not only for itself but also as a basis for justifying disengagement. Now he can legitimately focus on a circumscribed, more personal world.

What would Greg's life in Santa Fe be like? An earlier story, that of Max the potter, informs this question. Although Max was initially attracted to Santa Fe's *mañana* pace, he soon came to reject that aspect of it that involved smoking pot and "hanging out." It was a life without meaningful engagement, an existence filled with complacency and noncaring. He needed to purpose to define his life. Work had always provided this sense of mission; it pervaded and defined all of his activities. In coming to Santa Fe, the content of work happened to change to pottery, but the style and the consuming quality of work remained.

For Greg, work is similarly a way of life, a total defining force in living. He too will have to confront the hidden cost of Santa Fe's tempo. It may get to him and he will have to leave. It is not easy, being one of those determined people needing to accomplish something. Or if he chooses to stay, he will probably reconstruct the pace to suit his needs, by making his art work all-consuming and by refusing to accept any distinction between work and leisure.

But how likely is Greg to disengage from career and morality for a more personal life as an artist in Santa Fe? I don't think it is probable. He, like Max, voices a sense of moral indignation against the Establishment. In Max's situation, his voice had no impact; his immoralist—the academic and research establishment that excluded people because of their personality, not their lack of competence—did not yield. Had that structure bent, been less immoral, Max would likely have stayed in his career as an embryologist. Being a potter and coming to Santa Fe thus became an acceptable but not necessarily a preferred option. In a similar way, if corporate life would change toward Greg's views, he would probably shelve Santa Fe as a future option and continue the work that defines his life's meaning and purpose. For the foreseeable future, even if corporate life does not dramatically change, Santa Fe will still remain only a theoretical choice. He can still gain satisfaction in confronting corporate life. This has not been totally frustrated. His career still offers enough maneuverability to be exciting. For all his denial that crisis is a necessary component for making a radical shift, it is unlikely that he will do more than toy with the possibility of a move until the frustration of his eventual career limitations has reached impetus force.

These are some of my conjectures about Greg's future in Santa Fe. But what of Greg's wife, Nancy? She is at the beginning of a career, yet her work life seems to play a minor role in Greg's cost accounting. She is almost totally absent in the decision-making process except in giving tacit permission for Greg to act unilaterally. What would her life in Santa Fe be like?

Part of the answer is suggested by the next story. Fran's situation is not atypical of the unclear trajectory of work and living that many women living in Santa Fe experience. In her six years in Santa Fe she had to confront the difficult issues of marriage, career, and purpose. Santa Fe seemingly made it easy for her to avoid dealing with these problems. And this ease provided one of the sources of her subsequent discontent, a sense of purposelessness that finally led her to leave.

A similar set of reasons led Barry, whose story follows Fran's, to leave Taos. For all the communality of their dissatisfactions, their personal and cultural histories are dramatically different. A comparison of their lives provides the beginnings of an understanding of why some people choose not to stay in Santa Fe.

Tight Spaces

Fran's Story

The traffic going into San Francisco was heavy. As I edged along, I kept wondering why I didn't take 280. At least then I wouldn't be strangled by the industrial stench, by the blight of factories and plasticized motels. What a lot of aggravation for an interview.

I finally arrived at Fran's office. It was in a section of San

Francisco that the city fathers hoped would renew itself. An area of warehouses being renovated as artists' lofts and office spaces. A place of decaying hotels disgorging men who had no connection with the clean, soaring architecture of nearby proper San Francisco.

On the way to lunch, we walked past many of these vestiges of what once was, being pushed along by the midday crowd. The restaurant was packed, mostly with men, milling around, displaying their plumage.

"I hope you don't mind homosexuals," she said as we raced toward a vacant table. "It's about the only worthwhile place to eat around here," she explained as we squeezed into our hard-won place.

The noise level was deafening. She asked me, I think, how I had located her. She wasn't clear from our earlier phone conversation. I screamed over the noise that while I was in Santa Fe a few months back, I had seen Fred Lacey again. "He suggested I look you up."

"What did Fred say about me?" Fran's voice emerged above a nearby shout to pass the salt.

"I had sent him a copy of my manuscript on radical career changers in Santa Fe," I replied. "He felt I should have used his story or at least presented the point of view that his life in Santa Fe represented."

"Did you go out to his place? It's special."

"I stopped out there before I left. I like it too. It seems orchestrated for Fred—quiet, peaceful, sort of detached from the world."

"Did you get to see the sunset there?" Fran asked. "It's spectacular. I always tried to be home at sunset. My place was a little outbuilding just down the road from Fred's. Did you see it? I hope it hasn't crumbled away. Being that far out of town, it was so open, so peaceful, you could get in touch with yourself by getting into that red glow."

"No, I was out there in the morning. It was pretty calm then too. Anyway, Fred said that his major concern about my research was that I left the impression that the people I studied had found a reasonable solution in Santa Fe. He felt that I was being shortsighted. These people were only copping out on living, not solving their problems. He kept on talking about creative solutions for the problems of living. He saw Santa Fe as a place that almost made it simple to cop out, to stop confronting the real issues, like work, human relationships, sexuality, the whole thing."

"I think he's right. But I'm not sure it's that simple."

"That's why he told me to look you up. He said that you had fallen into the trap of Santa Fe but you were strong enough to get out, to innovate a special place for yourself."

"I sound very heroic. I had a rough time coming to grips with myself in Santa Fe. It took me two years of real pain, and a lot of sunsets on the ranch, to see what was happening. I wonder what Fred will think when he hears that I may be coming back to Santa Fe?"

Fran broke into a wry smile, thinking some private thought. It was the first break in the tension that seemed to cover her. I was a bit shocked by Fran's statement. "Why are you going back?" I asked with a note of disbelief.

"I have as much trouble with the idea as you seem to have. It isn't definite yet. My boyfriend and I are going out for three months this summer, to see if we like it, or I guess more whether we can find a way of making a living. Then we'll see."

"What is it that's drawing you back to Santa Fe?"

"I've thought a lot about why I want to go back. I know that I want to try Santa Fe again, but I'm not sure what the reasons are. Part of it is this—look around." Fran turned her chair around to face the restaurant. Her edginess increased. "When I came to San Francisco two years ago, I got turned on by watching raving queens like the one near the bar." Her eyes pointed to a tall man dressed in tight-fitting clothes, engaged in a highly animated conversation with the bartender. "I was excited by all the possibilities that San Francisco had to offer. This is an exciting place. Lots of interesting people, not too different from Santa Fe. But now I feel like it's closing down on me. There are just too many people, too much happening. There's not enough open space, no place to escape, to be free."

Our food arrived. Fran talked excitedly to the waitress. Something about an organization that they both belonged to. As best as I could figure out, they were involved in counseling battered women. The waitress left and Fran explained.

"I met Ruth a couple of months ago. We got together one day while I was having lunch. Sometimes this place isn't as much of a scene as it is today. She told me she had gotten involved with this women's organization. They had helped her deal with her husband, who was beating up on her all the time. Then she started to counsel other women who had the same problem. I got involved because I have always enjoyed working with women. It's like what happened in Santa Fe. One of the best things for me, at least workwise, was helping women who wanted to have natural childbirth."

"Let's go back for a minute. How do you explain your changed feelings about San Francisco? Why do you feel boxed in?"

"It's a lot of things. I haven't sorted out the pieces yet. One really important thing is my job. I guess it's my curse to be a good administrator. I seem to always end up doing that kind of work. Sure, my job is OK. I've worked myself up from being a lackey to running, pretty much, the whole operation. We're involved with city government and businesses, trying to find jobs for young kids, particularly the kind of kids no one wants to hire. Some have been in trouble with the police, or they are just plain disadvantaged. But this isn't what I want; this isn't what I left Santa Fe for."

"What was it that you were looking for?"

"I wasn't sure when I left Santa Fe. I'm not sure even now. But I'm sure it's not this. You see, I came to Santa Fe with my now ex-husband. We both had good jobs in New York. The rat race finally got to be too much. I didn't like my job;

from teacher to assistant principal in three easy but miserable years. After five years of working, I had had it. Dick, my ex-husband, had been ready to go for a long time. He figured out, pretty early on, that city planning and New York City were not for him. We headed off with no special place in mind. We stopped in Santa Fe and fell in love with it. Whatever it was about Santa Fe, it was enough for me to take a real crummy job. Dick seemed happy enough doing construction work, but I really hated my work. He persuaded me, without too much trouble, to give up the job. Then we had a daughter. Then we split up. We had been in Santa Fe two years by then.

"Here I was—twenty-nine years old—with a small kid, all alone, no job, and a little alimony. There were a lot of women like me in Santa Fe. I went on welfare and did the Santa Fe trip. Lots of friends, and a lot more self-exploration. The center of my life was me. I studied everything—astrology, leather work, *I Ching*, macrobiotics, all kinds of therapy. That's the way I met Fred and found that little house. You can learn a lot about yourself in six years, but also not know some really important things.

"I fell into a comfortable pattern. There were good friends who understood and shared in my problems. My ex-husband was there and could help with the baby. I loved the openness and the spirituality of the landscape. There were only two things wrong. The big thing was that I was lonely, even with all the friends. That kind of loneliness had kept me from leaving New York when I was single.

"What made me feel alone was not having an authentic relationship with a man. That's very important to me. Sure, there were lots of men floating around Santa Fe. But their trouble was that they're wanderers, emotionally immature guys who wanted nothing to do with commitment. Santa Fe is a lousy place for a single woman.

"The other problem was finding work. Welfare held things together financially. But I had to give it up when I got a small inheritance from my grandmother. Not big enough to make life comfortable, but it managed to get me off welfare. Anyway, it was also time to get off the dole. I had to get back to work because I was getting restless. I was nervous that I couldn't do it. I hadn't worked for three years. I was lucky. I got a job as a part-time bookkeeper. At least I had a job. I didn't like the work, but I proved to myself that I could work.

"But I was still restless. I wasn't peaceful inside even in that peaceful world. I wasn't being creatively satisfied. I dreamed of combining work with my need to be fulfilled. I figured that out at least two years before I let go of Santa Fe. I was just too comfortable, grooving along with all my friends who seemed satisfied with the Santa Fe trip. I finally got up the courage and decided to leave, with my daughter, for San Francisco. I figured I needed a bigger world to find myself. So I did the comfortable thing. While I was sitting in my little house in Santa Fe I applied to graduate school in Berkeley. I didn't get in. But then I decided I might as well try San Francisco anyway."

The noise level was lowering. People were leaving to return to wherever. "I'm getting a little tired of sitting" Fran said. "Do you feel like driving over the Golden Gate and hiking in the hills?"

I immediately agreed. I had been feeling claustrophobic since getting on the highway to San Francisco, and Fran's tension was communicable.

As we weaved our way through traffic, Fran asked, "Do you plan to settle in Santa Fe?"

"At one time I did. That was something I badly wanted," I answered. "I even tried to start a college as my meal ticket. It was an intellectual success but a financial disaster. I figured out the same thing you did. I needed to feel fulfilled creatively, and that wasn't going to happen by the landscape or my friends. Being a waiter or a desk clerk was too high a price to pay to live in Santa Fe."

"You're probably right. Unless I can find the right kind of job in Santa Fe, my boyfriend and I are going to search out another place. Maybe there is a 'right' place."

"If you find it, let me know. I've been looking for it all my life." We smiled at each other.

We started over the bridge. We had left the sun of San Francisco and entered the twilight zone of the span. The fog caressed the soaring reddish girders. Ahead we could see the sun sparkling, playing on the farthest supports. Rolled lengths of fog, suspended in the bright sunlight, squeezed between the distant hills.

We turned off the main highway and climbed a narrow road into the hills above the bridge. Fran began to relax. She said, mostly to herself, "This is a lovely place. I don't feel closed in here." She turned to me and said, "But this is not where I live. I live over there." She pointed to the city sitting off in the distance. High towers moving on different levels of hills, surrounded by water. For most, a landscape of gracious beauty. For Fran, and now for me, looking through her eyes, a world where the levels had collapsed on themselves, leaving no space.

"I have to try Santa Fe again," Fran said. "I've grown a lot here. I think I understand myself better now and what I want. I will never settle for a job just to keep alive."

"What is it that you want? What would be the single 'right' job, if you found it?"

"I'm not completely sure. I think it's important to let things happen, evolve naturally. I don't think I'm just floating into a job or into Santa Fe without some good reasons, some understanding of what I'm about. I fell into that trap when I left New York and landed up in Santa Fe. I think I'm past my old cop-out. You know, most girls are brought up expecting to be taken care of. It's so subtle, but it was very much part of me until I came to San Francisco. Here I was entirely by myself. Now I know I can make it. I can also deal with loneliness. All my life I was told it was important for little girls to be sociable, have lots of friends. Of course, don't be too smart. That doesn't make friends or catch a husband. So loneliness was pretty frightening. I don't like being alone. I don't think anyone wants it. It's really important to me to find someone I love to be with. But I think I can deal with loneliness."

We parked the car and started climbing a rocky trail.

"What about trying to create a job in Santa Fe for yourself?" I asked. "From what you've said, you seem to get a lot of fulfillment from working with women. Maybe . . ."

Fran broke in. "I feel a real kinship with women. I have a sense of political worth working with them. I've always wanted to be involved in something important. The women's thing is really important. Not like the bureaucratic crap I do. That's not what I want. I just want to believe that it is."

"Well, maybe you can put something together with some of the therapists in Santa Fe around women's problems?"

"It's funny, but I've just started thinking about that. For some reason I always thought in terms of established jobs. That's why I always land back in administration. It's so hard to break old patterns. In all my years of college, of learning to think critically, no one ever talked about things like how to think creatively about living."

We kept climbing. Winded, we sat down on a grassy hillside. All that we could see were hills growing into other hills. San Francisco had disappeared, and Fran seemed to be finally at peace.

Far Away, Near Enough

Barry's Story

Barry's desk was strewn with photographs, designs, and mock-ups. The quiet of his office was occasionally punctuated by the sounds of typewriters, phones, and voices. Sounds mag-

nified by the acoustics of a high-ceilinged space without walls
or partitions. Only tellers' cages and ponderous safes, standing
open, created any privacy for working.

Barry was the design editor of a local paper quartered in this
old bank biulding in a small old town near San Francisco. The
paper began as an underground throwaway. It was now becoming an aboveground success. Somehow the intact old bank
building, circa 1905, expressed Barry's calm but active movements.

I was waiting for Barry to finish a project. I observed a
handsome man. The beginning of gray in his hair added to
the aura of gentle intensity. The deepening lines in his face
expressed a life filled with a little too much worldly experience.

He looked up from his desk, shuffling the disorder into
disarray. I said, "It looks like you've come full circle. You're
back to your former career."

"In a way. I'm not sure I ever left it. After almost fifteen
years of bumming around, working at all sorts of weird things,
I realized that I never left the art world. That's why I hesi-
tated when you called me. I'm not sure I fit the category of
radical career changer."

"Given that few people fit it exactly, your history seems
right. You had an established career as a graphic designer and
then gave it up. You went to Taos and opened up a restaurant.
You also did some kind of group psychotherapy. You were
there for six years before you came out here. Is that a reasonable description?"

"It's right only in the very broadest outline. There was a
lot of in-between stuff, important things that happened."

"That's why I came up to see you. To fill in the details.
Also to find out why you left Taos. Would you mind if we
start talking about your original career and what made you
leave it? Oh, first, a minor question: How old are you?"

"I'm forty-two. Is this the interview? How do we do it?"

"Well, you construct the interview. I'll start it and then
you talk. I'll come in at points. Those that are unclear to me

or that I'd like to follow up in more detail. Let's start with your former career."

"OK. I worked as a graphic artist for about six years in Pittsburgh. Then I decided to chuck it. I wasn't doing much art work. I was more involved in the business end. That was the problem, or at least one of them. I was more of an account executive, handling about half a million dollars in business. I didn't like the responsibility. I didn't like being so far away from my art work.

"I was fine for the first few years, but things started to fall apart. I started to drink heavily. I had a lot of pressure at the job and even more from all the money I was making. Here I was, twenty-nine, with a wife, two kids, a big house in the suburbs with heavy mortgage payments, the whole bit. The thirty thousand dollars a year I was clearing—and that was a lot of money in 1964—never seemed to be enough. I didn't feel that there was much in all of this for me. I didn't know what I wanted, but I was getting pretty sure that I didn't want all this. My marriage also was going bad. Our communication was breaking down."

"About what? Was it about your work situation?" I interjected.

"That was one part of it. I started talking more and more about giving up my job and going back to school. At that time I had the dream of getting an M.F.A. and teaching art. But my wife didn't want to understand. Life was too comfortable for her. But it wasn't only the job that was between us. Everything else was falling apart too."

"So you chucked it all and went out to Taos?"

"No. That came later. I broke up with my wife and went back to school. I finished my B.F.A. in a year and a half and got an assistantship for the M.F.A. program. But that started falling apart too. I had gotten screwed in the divorce settlement. I had heavy alimony payments since the court computed it on the basis of my old job. So I was barely surviving. Trying to put together a life, doing something that I began to see I didn't want. I wanted to be an artist, not a teacher. I couldn't take being a student either. To top it all off, I re-married. Why, I don't know.

"I had a friend who was going through a similar thing. So we decided to go off, you know, for the big adventure—off to California. My wife was with us. We stopped off in Taos to see the D. H. Lawrence ranch since my buddy had written a paper on it. That was the end of the trip. We decided that this was the place."

"What was it about Taos?"

"How do you describe it in words? You really have to paint it. It's the light and the color. The openness. You can see all around. A real feeling of space. That's the best I can do.

"Anyway, after a few months our money was beginning to run out. So we decided to open a restaurant. A pizza place. It's still there, behind the hotel on the plaza. Have you eaten there?"

"No, but I've passed it."

"I didn't know anything about pizza, but I learned. I guess you'd call that a radical career change. But the restaurant was just a way to keep alive so that I could do my art work. I had gotten back into painting by that time.

"I also started getting into drugs. I got turned on by the things the kids were doing there—building solar houses, living up in the mountains, and doing the whole drug trip. When I dropped acid, everything changed."

"How?"

"I got a perspective on my life. I can't explain it. I just realized that my friend—he was my partner in the restaurant —was becoming middle class, a real small-businessman type. He was getting compulsive about the business and there was a lot of friction about it. And my wife was also a little too straight. She couldn't take my hip life. So I started acting out even more. That ensured that we'd split. I guess that's what I wanted but couldn't confront openly.

"I had to hit bottom before my life could clear up. That

happened when I went back to Pittsburgh. I had been missing my kids, so I went home. I got a job as a cabbie and tried to paint in my off time. I started feeling trapped, just like I did when I was working as a graphic artist. I was by then heavy into the dope trip. I was pretty wasted and I knew it. I knew I had to get it put together. Finally, I got busted for having grass.

"I was let out on probation. About that time, I met a friend who was doing Reichian therapy in New York. I went with him. I guess I needed a safe place. I wasn't much interested in the therapy stuff. Actually, now I can see that I was scared about what I might find out about myself.

"But I got involved, first as a client and then running groups. I got my act together and was ready to go back to Taos, to try it again."

"How long were you away?"

"About a year and a half, maybe closer to two. I was living with a woman at the time and she came out with me. I hadn't realized how much I had changed until I got there. Taos was still the same place I had left. It really hadn't changed much in the two years I was gone. But I was a different person coming back.

"Like, by that time, I was really into my art work. I was also involved in Reichian therapy, running about five groups a week. But I also wanted to be involved in Taos. So I started working on community projects. But the community stuff was just fragmenting me. My guts were in the art work and the therapy. Taos was a bad place to be a professional. It's isolated. Not much stimulation. I didn't have anyone around to talk to about my Reichian work. The local therapists were either into a conservative psychoanalytic number or into a lot of off-the-wall techniques. And I didn't find much to push against in my art work. Most of the Taos artists were at a different place, working on problems that didn't interest anyone. They weren't in touch with the things going on in New York or anywhere else where new art was happening. They had cut themselves off from the outside. And that was the way I was feeling. I wanted to get on with my professional life, and Taos wasn't the right place for that."

"Is that why you came out here?"

"Partly. I probably would have stayed on. I was getting settled in. I had been out there four years by then. But the real push to get out was my ladyfriend. We weren't getting along and she wanted to stay in Taos, and I didn't want to be anywhere near her. So I headed off.

"First I landed up in Berkeley. I had a friend from Taos living there. But Berkeley was a heavy place—too many people doing too many trips. So I got involved with some people who started this paper and moved up here. I like them and I like the town. This place hasn't yet been overrun by the tourists. There are a lot of good people here, mostly artists and craftsmen doing their own work. I'm learning a lot, and I'm back to doing graphics and painting, which is where I started out fifteen years ago. But now I'm happy with it."

"You've been through a lot," I commented. "I wonder about one thing. One of the guys I interviewed pointed out that Santa Fe, or Taos, can be a stultifying place. People get so comfortable that they never really confront themselves. How do you feel about this, looking back at your years in Taos?"

"I see it as relative. Like with the kids out there. I saw them, when I first came out, as really having a grasp on things. When I came back I saw them as copping out on living, not really connected with the world. Part of how I saw them may have been them, what they were doing. But a lot of it had to do with how I had changed. I needed Taos the first time. It was a backdrop for me to work out a lot of my stuff. The second time I didn't need a stage any more. So it depends on what perspective you are coming from."

"Do you have any desire to go back?"

"Sure, I still love the place, but not for the old reasons. Now I'm at a time when I need to learn and work. Here I'm close enough to the art action, the museums, the artists who are working on new problems. I have what I need. I'm not hassled by the action; it's peaceful up here, far away but close enough.

"I see those years in Taos as what I needed at that time, as part of a process. I couldn't be here if I hadn't been there. When I'm put together I can be anywhere. I'm not sure where I'm going from here, but I'm sure that being in this bank and working on the newspaper is a necessary stage leading somewhere."

"That's a philosophy I've heard in New Mexico a number of times. It that where you picked it up?"

"Maybe. It's just the way I can make some sense out of my life. Sometimes I think about it in another way. If you're painting a picture, you try to get everything in balance and harmony. You might have to change something really good because it doesn't fit. You work on it till it's right, till you feel comfortable with it. I feel comfortable with my life now. I've changed some of the pieces, shifted others. I may have to change it again when things get out of balance, even some of the good things. But that's OK. The place you're in, whether it's Taos or New York, is really the frame for the picture. Some people mistake it for the painting. But what has to be worked on is the painting, and that's you."

We talked some more, mostly about common friends in New Mexico. Barry asked me, as he was about to leave for a meeting, "Where are you with Santa Fe?"

I answered, "To use your imagery, I don't need that frame anymore, but I'm not sure what the right frame is. Perhaps the process will make that clear. But first I guess I have to get comfortable with the idea of living as a process."

Fred Lacey uses Fran's life to illustrate how destructive Santa Fe's psychological comforts could be. He elevates her leaving to near-heroism; she had managed the strength to fight the inertia of her life. Santa Fe is a costly environment, and

Fran refused to pay the price for remaining. She could now get on with living. Fred could reasonably cite Barry's life as additional evidence for his interpretation.

However, his view has a number of hidden assumptions. He tacitly maintains that through confronting oneself, an individual eventually arrives at a creative resolution to his dilemmas. This resolution has the quality of being a right answer, a final, ultimate conclusion to the questions of living. Measured against this answer, all events and experiences that do not directly and positively contribute to the end point are of little value. Thus Santa Fe's comforts and supports block confrontation, becoming distractions, deflections away from the trajectory of creative resolution. At best, Santa Fe is a transitional world from which the individual can approach his goal. At worst, it is an all-too-pleasant nowhere that can be mistaken for a meaningful somewhere.

But Fran's and Barry's lives in New Mexico can be interpreted in another way. It is an interpretation that is implicit in their own description. (The same view can be found in the earlier stories of Mark and Mike.) From their point of view, the Santa Fe–Taos environment is not simply a place for pleasant inactivity, but also a setting that allows for confrontation and growth. These encounters with self admittedly can be destructive, like Barry's plummeting decline into the drug culture, or Fran's loss of self-confidence. But they are still confrontations, a basis for evaluating needs and goals. The comfort and support in the environment need not block such encounters, as Fred Lacey maintains. The environment may structure and define the issues. It often provides support for the confrontation. Many encounters with self would likely not happen if there were not such supporting environments. But to place the blame for nonconfrontation on Santa Fe would be to mistake the frame for the picture, the setting for the individual.

This interpretation forms one part of the underlying logic by which Fran and Barry define their lives. This logic does not have the defined form of Fred Lacey's "creative resolution"; it is more loosely structured. It is governed by an unclear, amorphous force called "process." Its stress is upon the present moment as experienced, rather than the present distilled through some future goals and meanings.

The unfolding of process often takes the form of seemingly unrelated, perhaps insignificant events that are interpreted as necessary for the emergence of later options. For example, while Barry was involved in the drug scene during his first Taos period, he interpreted his experience as being both positive in leading to some clarity about his life, and negative in leading ultimately to his arrest. But looking back at these experiences, he now interprets them as being at the root of his commitment to art and therapy. Fran originally viewed her comfortable withdrawal into self and into friends as an enjoyable period of living. Now she sees that time as a prerequisite for her present reassessment of work and career.

In the logic of process, an individual's solutions are not final, nor is there one correct trajectory. Process provides the experiences from which the individual can then select. The particular content of a person's experience is left open to possibility and without any imposition of control or definition. By taking this unstructured attitude, the person can grasp situations as they make themselves available.

Whatever the chance quality of process, Fran's and Barry's relationship to their lives' logic is not passive. There are certain priorities that they actively maintain and that structure their selection of possibilities. Within the boundaries of these significant meanings and priorities, process is allowed to operate freely. In Barry's case, the fixed priority has always been work. In giving up his original career, he did not withdraw from his art work. He just left the account-executive setting for it. His later involvement with the pizza restaurant was not a radical shift in career but rather a means to sustain his work. Even his withdrawal from work, during his first Taos period, is interpreted as a basis for a later renewed commitment to work; he had to live through his "adolescent fantasy" so that he could subsequently reject the Taos setting for a more professional environment. Within the unbending boundaries of his work priority, he then can grasp the possibilities presented by personal interactions. In Barry's life, human relationships do not have a high priority. He seems to use people in an instrumental way, when his need dictates their presence. Relationships have a transitory quality; his wives and lovers have a faceless, interchangeable appearance; his many friends somehow appear when needed. In many ways Barry resembles the men Fran disliked in Santa Fe, people who were committed to being uncommitted in relationships.

In contrast, Fran's fixed priority is upon relationship, the aspect that Barry leaves open to process. For Fran, an authentic relationship with a man must be obtained before work can be meaningfully considered. Her decision to leave Santa Fe, for instance, although defined in work terms, seems more likely a function of a lack of available men. Having now established an authentic relationship in San Francisco, she can consider returning to Santa Fe. That relationship provides the basis from which she can more actively engage the issues of work, an arena she has traditionally left open to process. By taking this passive stance, she somehow alway found herself as an adminstrator. Now she is trying to make her work world less open to process by actively structuring it into a stable, fixed priority. But she is still unsure whether she is in control of her decision to structure her work and return to Santa Fe. She fears making another aimless move; "process" cannot inform her concern. She cannot totally accept that, even with her beginning redefinition of work's priority, relationships are still at the center of her life and that they provide the real justification of what otherwise would be a pointless change. She knows that Santa Fe is likely not be the "right" place to find fulfillment in work; she has already experienced its problematic economic realities. But she must return. Santa Fe contains many compelling forces of being "at home"—friends, a physical environment in which she feels free, and a sense of being meaningfully embedded. Had work truly assumed a top priority in Fran's life, there would be little justification for returning. She sees her work of helping women as meaningfully associated with the Santa Fe environment. Work, relationship, and environment have now become inextricably entwined as a general priority in her life. This view is in marked contrast to that of Barry, who has no need to return to Taos. His work is still primary, and is unrelated to particular relationships or settings except insofar as they sustain his work priority.

One explanation for the difference between Fran's and Barry's priorities and overarching meanings lies in our culture's differential socialization of men and women. Whatever the reason, their different priorities share the character of defining the important goals for their lives. Their specific form is left, from Barry's and Fran's point of view, to the operation of process. There is no one final creative resolution, but rather a series of renegotiated goals and needs. In these terms, there is no fixed price to living in Santa Fe. The cost of coming or of remaining is inherent neither in the environment nor in the individual but in some interaction between the setting and the person's needs at a particular juncture of living.

The underlying logic that Fran and Barry see operating in their lives cannot be evaluated as being either right or wrong. It is simply their means of ordering and interpreting experience. Its value can be gauged by how functional it is, how effective it is in making sense of their world. It is only one among many structures, many interpretive frameworks, by which an individual can impose meaning on his life.

COLLAPSING FRAMES

Soon after completing my interviews, I presented my findings to an audience of mental health professionals. After the talk, a middle-aged man approached me and made the following comment, a statement I soon learned was going to be a consistent and predictable reaction to my research. "Sure, I'd like to go to Santa Fe," he said. "I've wanted to pull out of the mess of my life. My catalog of woes is as good as your 'radical career changers.' But I don't let myself think about it, at least not too often. Why should I? I just can't pull out and do what I want. I have a lot of responsibility. My kids are growing up and need things. At work, for all its aggravations, I have a lot of people who are dependent on me, and I feel that I am responsible to accomplish something with my life. Going to Santa Fe is not a real option for me.

"And another thing. You keep skirting a very important question. What I'd like to know is 'Are these people happy with their lives?' "

The tone of his comments, and the many similar ones that I encountered, conveyed a sense of subdued anger, bred of frustration in knowing (or believing) that he had no choice but to remain in what was a problematic, almost crisis-level, life situation.

At one time, I had a ready-made reply to such comments. I simply answered with the radical career changers' argument that remaining back home is likely to be more costly than making a radical change. Moreover, they seemed happy. By acting on this position, they had found, I believed, a reasonable solution to their "back home" concerns—they had left most of them behind. Santa Fe and radical change had taken on for me the rosy glow of a refuge in a troubled world.

I now find their answers too simple and my acceptance un-critical. Yet, a number of important questions raised by their viewpoint and experience must be confronted if any sense is to be made out of a search for a meaningful life. I'd like to develop, in some detail, the radical career changers' position so that these issues can be clarified.

For them, the range of perceived choice was as narrow as that of the middle-aged questioner. But they saw the restriction of their options as the reason and basis for revamping their entire structure of choice.

The radical career changer believes that if he had remained in his "back home" situation, his life would have become one of quiet desperation. All the previous stories indict the people back home who refuse to confront the problems of their present lives. The charge was put most pointedly by the forty-three-year-old former social service administrator turned welfare recipient and jack-of-all-trades: "People thought I was absolutely crazy for doing it, but I think they're crazy for staying where they are. Some people said that they wished they had the opportunity to do what I was doing. Well, they have the same choice. They'll have to suffer—hustling to eke out an existence. But too many people are frightened—that need for security. They have all sorts of excuses, but it's really inertia and a lack of courage to do something. The thing that's really frightening is that a lot of them don't see what would be obvious to anyone who examined his life. They don't want to see the futility of their own existence, because to look at that would mean to confront themselves."

The indictment is clear: the cost of leading the unex-amined life is to experience only a part of living. Moreover, "back home" does not offer the full range of possibilities for a fulfilling life. What those possibilities include is not clear to the radical career changer. They are what he is searching for.

But the absence of possibilities is easier to detect. It is sig-naled in more or less obvious ways: sometimes vaguely, as Fran

experienced it—a gnawing, undefinable sense of incomplete-
ness, a lack of fulfillment—often more overtly. A thirty-eight-
year-old former insurance agent turned construction worker
described his experience of dramatically clear indicators of
emptiness: "I was the great American dream. I had made my
first million when I was thirty-two. The Junior Chamber of
Commerce elected me executive of the year. But my life
wasn't right. I couldn't figure it out. That's not to say I tried
very hard. The booze made sure of that. No, I explained
getting bombed all the time as just part of my job. A couple
of drinks to make a sale. A little social drinking at night.
Everyone around me was getting bombed too. That's a Texas
habit. Also, I was breaking my butt working so that I could
buy, buy, buy. I had everything and more than I or anyone
could want, but I had to buy.

"I saw what was happening in those couple of months I
spent alone in the desert. I went there to dry out and medi-
tate, after some friends and I got involved in the civil rights
movement back home. Our lives had been threatened, and I
saw the great American dream and me for what it was—not
much. I pulled out and went to the desert to think. From
there I understood that I was an alcoholic and a compulsive
buyer because I had to fill a big hole in my life. The booze
and the property made up for it, but not very well. They
couldn't really make up for holding still, living with a frigid
wife, and working at a job that was simply ripping people off."

Given the choice between such a futile, unexamined life
and the risky option of immigrating to Santa Fe, the decision
was self-evident, although arriving at the point of making that
choice was often agonizing. What made the decision less difficult was defining all other alternatives as implausible or even
ridiculous. The restriction of choice, where Santa Fe becomes
the only sensible option, has been hinted at by Greg's cost
accounting. In evaluating his choices, using his moral stand as
a criterion, he eliminates the options of remaining at work,
changing jobs, or trading off work for leisure. By giving himself permission to withdraw from moral confrontation, he

finds his only acceptable choice is to go to Santa Fe. Such a restriction of choice can be seen, with different degrees of clarity, in all the preceding stories.

The clearest illustration of this narrowing is provided by the previously quoted former social service administrator: "What I wanted to do was to provide services that people needed and wanted. But what did I do—I spent most of my time being nice to rich people so that they would support the agency. What really started to frighten me was that I was getting to be like them. In this town in Oklahoma, most people spend their time drinking, hunting, and traveling. Everybody has a fair amount of money. It was a big oil town and everybody was on the make. I got to be on the make, and I didn't like what I was seeing about myself.

"My frustration must have really shown itself, because I came in increasing conflict with the board of directors. I realized what I was doing. I had advanced in the social work field and began to understand that it was the same everywhere. I was going places, but I didn't like most of the places. Finally what put an end to this whole progression was the day when a couple of the directors came into my office, sat down, and noted that I had the *New Republic* on my coffee table. This was a bit risqué for the arch-conservative Birchites. I had had it by that point, and by mutual consent, neither the board nor I being too unhappy about my choice, I decided to leave.

"So what was I to do? I could have gone back to school, retooled for a new career. But I couldn't take the academic structure before, and then, being thiry-five, I was sure I couldn't put up with it at all. Anyway, what I wanted to be was a college teacher. And it was a bad time to get a job doing that. I really didn't want to start over from scratch. I could have gotten another social agency job. There were a lot of good openings, and I had a growing national reputation. But they all had the same problem as the job I just left. The only real option was to pull out and begin a new life where I could be independent."

The loss of his job did not produce a crisis. Rather it precipitated an awareness of the crisis he had been living but refused to examine. His life and choices were then put under scrutiny and found shallow and meaningless. The mode of coming to that awareness differs with each person interviewed. For some, it arose out of the discontinuity created by job loss or divorce. For others it appeared simply from taking the opportunity to reflect and examine.

For instance, a forty-six-year-old former stockbroker who became a shopkeeper came to his realization in the middle of a traffic jam: "I was sitting in my car at a dead halt. It would take me, as usual, nearly an hour to go the four miles to the office. Why did I need this crap? So I made a lot of money. For what? To support a household that was more than I wanted and needed. So my kids could go to a good school. But I didn't like the values they were learning and the kinds of people they were becoming. My marriage was falling apart at the seams, partly because of the job, but mostly because of us. That traffic jam was really valuable. It gavē me time to see in some perspective that my life was crumbling. That's when I seriously started thinking about what I could do."

Whatever the source of perspective, all the obtained insights came from taking a fresh, almost naive look at the world and concluding that "things don't necessarily have to be this way." Given the critical distance from which to evaluate their lives, the radical career changers could entertain the important and difficult next step of accepting the possibility that they could change their lives, that their present and future need not be like their past. Max's story makes clear some facets of assessing the possibility of change. The idea that he was a free agent originally surfaced at an inauspicious time—when his life was in order and he had no desire to change it. He was willing to entertain that somewhat threatening thought only when he lost his funding and was unable to find an acceptable job.

Why did Max find the idea that he was a free agent so difficult to handle? It is the very same reason that stops most people from considering the option of Santa Fe. As an idea, it throws into sharp relief how real are an individual's choices. For Max, as for most of us, the notion seems paradoxical, since we define ourselves in the role of being responsible individuals. Part of work's value, as our society defines and as we introject, is that it provides the basis for fulfilling our responsibility—feeding, clothing, and sheltering ourselves and our families. In turn, responsibility provides an easy definition of our role in society and the basis for meaning in our lives. Why entertain the notion of free choice, many would say, since our responsibility makes that a hollow theoretical option? But the experience of the radical career changer suggests that choice is more open and that responsibility, while real and important, need not be a deterrent to finding a better life.

Responsibility weighed heavily in the radical career changers' considerations of giving up their careers and life styles. But the emerging crises in their lives made freedom of choice more than a theoretical option. They were forced to make decisions about the trajectory of their lives and in the process had to consider what were the nature and extent of their responsibilities. They saw that responsibility need not be constraining; that it is limiting only if one wants it to be; that it is often not a reason for lack of freedom, but an excuse. In coming to Santa Fe, each of them had to renegotiate his responsibilities, renegotiate in terms of how much was necessary for a reasonable, satisfactory life. While they maintained the ingredients of such a life—decent food, clothing, and shelter—its quality and quantity were reevaluated. The renegotiation varied in difficulty: some came with money, others were broke; some had little in the way of responsibilities, others had families to support, either in Santa Fe or back home; some acted without concern, leaving a wreckage of their former lives behind; others attempted to minimize the disruption their radical change could produce.

But to pass off the choice of changing a career as a function of seemingly lessened responsibility, as my middle-aged questioner implied, is to avoid the crucial question, namely, how much does an individual or a family need in order to maintain a satisfactory existence? Is an individual being responsible to himself or his family if he provides them with little more than the bare essentials of living? It is not that the radical career changers have purposely chosen to live minimally. They have the taste, the appetite, and often the desire for an expensive life from those previous years of affluent living. They are willing to live more simply since their incomes allow for little else. They were willing to give up their material goods since they found there was a more paramount value than an affluent life: the value of greater freedom from external constraints, which, in turn, allows them to feel free to be themselves.

This point is made graphically by a forty-eight-year-old former well-established filmmaker turned farmer: "Before I came out here, I didn't know what I wanted. It only became clear when I took the jump. What I wanted was to be independent, free to do films as I thought they should be done, not to cater to producers or to the customers. I'm willing to be a farmer if that's what it takes to be free of the bullshit. Now, if I get a film job, I tell them—they don't tell me—what is right. If they don't like it, I come back and farm."

The costs of obtaining this freedom involved more than a reevaluation of material possessions. It meant a redefinition of how to measure one's own personal value and the direction of a life. The new-found work in Santa Fe could not provide an adequate measure since, in most cases, work's major significance was to sustain the life the radical career changer chose to lead.

This presented a difficult problem for him: how to measure the success of a life when work is perceived as secondary to an evolving life style. Before changing his career, he, like most of us, used the available grading structure of work to evaluate the success of his life's direction. Getting a raise or promotion partially validates that one's work has been successful. But work interpenetrates and is not easily separable from other sectors of living; the spillover of moving through work's grading structure can also be found in other life activities. For example, such movement produces one basis for success in the family sector. The individual can use the increased benefits of his graded work to make a better life for his family. Work provides the wherewithal for acquiring more goods and experiences—travel, entertainment, property, schooling, and so on. For the radical career changer, work brought these benefits, and yet they were found to be empty. They did not bring personal satisfaction, and even tended to erode the nonwork world of family and interpersonal relationships.

Given the choice to leave his career, and with the limitations of work possibilities in the Santa Fe area, the radical career changer redefined (from choice or necessity) the significance of work as a measure of life. He was not often so free and independent as the film director turned farmer. He still lived within the constraints of welfare structures, his employment, or his buying public. But his attitude toward work had changed, making these boundaries less confining. This changed attitude is well summarized by the statement of a thirty-six-year-old Ph.D. computer scientist turned carpenter: "If I do go back to computer work, I will define my work, not let my work define me. That's what I've learned out here."

This statement implies a rejection of another important aspect of work. Work not only provides the grading structure to measure accomplishment, but also provides a definition of self. The standard equivalency of "Who are you?"—meaning "What do you do for a living?"—is no longer acceptable, or even applicable, to the radical career changer. The problem he still struggles with, as I discussed in the chapter "Dropping In, Dropping Out," is finding a more meaningful alternative to work's definition of self. In part, the emerging definitions of self are adapted from the values of Santa Fe—whether it is in relation to the landscape, or embeddedness in a sense of community, or in a less hurried, less technological life style. They have evolved a set of criteria for measuring their lives that is different from what they had back home. Those who haven't found a new source of definition in Santa Fe are searching for a new place to go.

Thus far, the radical career changers' argument has the particularistic quality of their own lives. Their questioning the meaning of responsibility, work, and choice acquires a fuller measure of power when their lives and concerns are placed in their natural embeddedness, namely, the culture in which they hold membership. In this broader context, the radical career changers' concerns become symptomatic of our culture's increasing inability to provide its members with adequate sources of meaning and ways of interpreting experiences.

Let me sketch in a few important facets of the relation between culture and the individual's ways of understanding his life. A person's place in a culture is simultaneously personal and social. While we own our meanings and dwell within a personal view of our experiences, we also recognize that this reality is not simply idiosyncratic. Our private world is understood and shared by other people. They and we are part of that communal world called "culture." While the individual contributes to defining his culture, he is, more significantly, defined by it. A culture provides its members with shared ways of interpreting experience through a system of symbols, meanings, values, standards, and rituals. Within the boundaries of what the culture defines as possible, the individual member is free (within limits of toleration) to construct his own psychological reality. Having this personal and shared perspective, the individual can then interpret his past, structure his present, and project his future.

We are more aware of our personal world since we live within it; our cultural definitions and boundaries are less accessible. They are almost invisible, being tacitly communicated in the process of childhood socialization, and are, in later life, assumed as a common basis of communication. The acts of interpreting experience, being continually operative and practiced, become habitual, almost reflexive. They require little cognitive awareness or conscious accessibility. In fact, such access is likely to disrupt their successful operation, just as an awareness of the movements involved in propelling a bicycle disturbs the normal flow of riding. In a similar way, the act of questioning the well-practiced ways of understanding experience makes the implicit explicit. In the process, the functional reflexivity of our interpretations can be disrupted, and a high degree of distress results until some interpretive structure is successfully reestablished.

The radical career changer chose to disrupt his interpretations by questioning his personal and shared view of work, among other meanings. To attack the value of work was to confront a paramount cultural value. As Simone Weil acutely commented: "Our age has it own particular mission, or vocation—the creation of a civilization founded upon the spiritual nature of work. The thoughts relating to a presentiment of this vocation, and which are scattered about in Rousseau, George Sand, Tolstoy, Proudhon and Marx, in papal encyclicals and elsewhere, are the only original thoughts of our time, the only ones we haven't borrowed from the Greeks." *

Yet, the radical career changer found this meaning unsatisfactory as a way to define his life. It was no longer functional in providing a coherence to his experience in the work domain and those areas where it shared interconnections. Through his doubt, he reinterpreted the past, assessed his present, and attempted to construct a more meaningful future. He experienced, in more than a metaphorical sense, a loss, or even a death, of former meanings. His problem was to resolve that loss and the concomitant distress. The search for a solution was thus more profound than simply finding a straightforward answer to such questions as what new career to pursue or how to apportion time between work and leisure. The needed resolution required him to evolve an alternative set of orderings for his experiences.

* *The Need for Roots* (London: Routledge, 1952), pp. 91–92.

Where could he turn for an answer, or at least for assistance and support? It became obvious that he couldn't rely on his culture: he had chosen to question and dismiss its values and boundaries. The evidence for his culture's rejection was compelling: his private world of questioned meanings was no longer shared by his friends back home. They became the representatives of the culture he was on the way to rejecting. His friends found his doubts and actions unintelligible: he was willing to give up their shared definitions and, therefore, them as well. They offered him little support; to entertain the legitimacy of his concerns might tip the precarious balance of their own ambivalence, which they had purposely avoided confronting.

The radical career changer could have stayed back home. This they all admitted. The interstices of that culture would allow them to establish an alternative life style. But they chose to relocate in Santa Fe, simply because it was "somewhere else." In Santa Fe there would be no painful reminders of a past life. Nor would there be much semblance of former values, of the culture of "back home." These were some of the hopes with which they approached Santa Fe.

Few knew, in a specific way, what Santa Fe held for them. At first, they saw what was on the surface and immediately accessible: a dramatic, powerful landscape and the exotica of the Spanish and Indian cultures. Soon after relocating, they found that Santa Fe was a unique and special "other place," that the boundaries of their search for new meanings and interpretations were gradually being structured by the particular nature of the setting.

Santa Fe dictated a radical career change—it could seldom be otherwise, for the economic realities were too harsh to reconstitute a former career. Although the radical career changer did not necessarily want to continue being a minister (or an editor or a professor), becoming a cook (or construction worker or school bus driver) was often a bit more extreme than he had expected. But if this was the price being exacted for rejecting cultural values and for being away from "back home," it was not too high to pay. In turn, the dramatic shift in work required that the meaning of status, career, and accomplishment be renegotiated. These concerns were not resolved but tended to recede in significance with the change from an affluent career-oriented life style to a humbler life of toil. The need to survive and maintain a life assumed priority over the more global concerns about meaning and purpose. The redefinition of meanings was also made easier because few people in Santa Fe seemed to care about such indices of success.

The radical career changer found that besides the more visible Indian and Spanish cultures was another culture—a world where he could find support and understanding. Santa Fe was a place that had drawn people like himself, people who were searching, people who had confronted themselves and their culture and still remained marginal to it. They were Chester's people, who had lived through loneliness, or Len's associates, who were willing to share in, but not intrude upon, his enthusiasms, or Barry's counterculture friends, who showed him the joys of being close to the land and the pleasures of the drug experience. It was a world rich in shared meanings and experiences.

Here was a world where the radical career changer's former marginality now became normative, a basis for constructing a different culture. He had ceased to be a threat to established boundaries.

Here was an environment where the disasters of "back home" technology had not yet fully arrived. The landscape was still relatively unsullied, the pace more sensible and human. It was a setting where the machine was often purposely rejected in favor of the hand, where adobe homes were to be shaped directly from the soil and food was to be carved from the arid, ungiving earth. The romance of the wilderness that had drawn generations of Americans to the frontier still lived in New Mexico. The joys of living this idyll, of enjoying solitude, of being independent and close to nature also had their painful and frightening sides. There was the real difficulty of surviving, of being marginal to the established Spanish and Indian cultures and to the land. But the price was not too high for being in such a special "somewhere else."

The outlines of the solution the radical career changer sought were ready-made in this new world. He had now to evolve his own private meanings, definitions, and interpretations, within the frame it provided.

Some have been more successful than others. Most have stayed; of those, some have carved a meaningful niche within the living landscape of Santa Fe; others have recreated a "back home" world of values and meanings, establishing continuities with their former lives, cloaked in "New Mexico Chic." Then there were those who left, those who found Santa Fe's boundaries either too open or too confining. But any definition of what is a successful adaptation to the Santa Fe world is partially illusory, especially if success is equated with happiness. The emerging cultural values are neither clear nor stable. Nor is the individual's adaptation to it static or unchanging. Moreover, in a culture that rejects "success" as an important criterion of a life's value, any judgment from within that culture must be personal and relative. Any judgment from outside these Santa Fe values is unclear in its implication.

In the sense that Santa Fe's cultural boundaries are fluid and in process, this world becomes a constantly changing personal space. The psychological reality of Santa Fe is like a movie screen on which the inhabitant projects his own picture show within the boundaries of the frame. As a physical location, Santa Fe is unique. It occupies a distinct geographical space, easily found on a New Mexico map. As a psychological world, it is almost interchangeable with many other places whose cultural boundaries are in process and are sufficiently different from "back home" to be a "somewhere else."

From the radical career changer's perspective the search for a meaningful life presents a stark, polarized choice. Either the person remains back home, futilely living within the narrow constraints of responsibility and problematic work, or he radically changes his life style, redefining responsibility and denying former sources of meaning in favor of new meanings to be evolved in the somewhere else of a Santa Fe out there. The midway alternatives of finding a different job or retooling for a new career become compromises that have the unfortunate aspects of both choices and none of the benefits of either.

The radical career changers' polarized alternatives seemed more than sensible to me when I was considering making a radical change myself. However, by the time of my college's economic failure, I had come to seriously question whether there was some other meaningful alternative, some solution that the radical career changers and I had somehow overlooked. I knew that the radical solution would not work for me. An essential element was missing in that extreme approach. I found it difficult to define, but it had something to do with my need for a defining structure and a discomfort with the kind of freedom that the *mañana* pace offered. It involved an increasing sense that I had a responsibility to accomplish something with my life.

What that something was was as unclear to me as it was to my middle-aged questioner or to Richard, who claimed that "there has to be more to living than doing what you want to do." I also had come to the recognition and acceptance that I couldn't provide someone like Chester with an answer, or even a direction, to his question of whether he was meant to be "a sort of happy, eccentric clockmaker in Santa Fe, living in a little ole cabin in the mountains with lots of ticktock, Mickey Mouse things." How could I answer him when I had no more understanding of my life's purpose than he? All I could offer him or myself were statements of what I wanted or, more often, what I didn't want. The solitude during the nights of my college's registration period—when nobody came to enroll—helped to define my growing awareness that I must continue searching for that elusive alternative between the radical career changers' polarized options.

As a beginning to that search, I returned to the adult development literature in the hope of finding an answer. It had served me well before in defining a context of interpretation for my dissatisfactions and those of the radical career changers. Perhaps it could now illuminate the dimensions of my present concerns.

On the surface, this growing literature promised a great deal. This knowledge will likely legitimate communication of what had been assumed to be only private. Thus, the person confronting his own questions of meanings and values may soon find, with the incorporation of this literature into the culture, support in knowing that he shares this experience and its distress with other people. New cultural boundaries may emerge within which such experiences can be accepted as legitimate rather than being expelled as "crazy," as a "personal problem."

There should also be comfort in knowing that not only is the experience widely shared but its causes are known and the shape of its future is definable and predictable. Such understanding fosters a sense of mastery of what seems inexplicable and uncontrollable. The need for Santa Fe could thus become a vestige of this particular time in American culture. The literature would make "back home" resemble "somewhere else." The searcher could now remain back home, finding support and understanding, and thus resolve his concerns without seeking or creating a new culture. Perhaps this is what Fred Lacey's "creative resolution" involved.

The adult development literature, at its poorest, can offer a consoling label to define, and perhaps explain, the problems of different stages in adult life. Like the term "the terrible two's," which describes (but does not really explain) the unexpected oppositional behavior of two-year-olds, the phrase to be coined—perhaps the "frightening forties"—may offer just enough knowledge as is needed to outwait the end of this difficult period. At its best, the literature can provide one way of understanding the changes that occur in an adult's life.

As I explored this way of understanding, I found it too narrow; there was a shallowness beneath the surface of the literature's promise. The writings of Philip Rieff and Ernest Becker helped me to define its character.*

To explore the limits of the adult development literature's directions in the search for meaning, I have created the following fictional but, I believe, representative dialogue between a client in midlife distress and his therapist. (This condensed interchange can also be viewed as the interaction between a thoughtful reader relating to the adult development literature.) After presenting their dialogue and the client's important concluding question (set off in italics), I have provided three possible responses that the therapist could make to this question. The analysis that follows each answer helps to define some of the issues involved in using the adult development frame of reference.

THERAPIST: What's troubling you?

CLIENT: It's hard to pinpoint. Mostly, I'm just depressed. Nothing seems to make a difference. I sit in my office, doing my work, and wonder why I'm bothering. Everything seems meaningless.

THERAPIST: Do you usually enjoy your work?

CLIENT: Sometimes. It's easier to take it when I can turn off thinking.

THERAPIST: Thinking about what?

CLIENT: A lot of disconnected things. Mostly, what's this all about?

THERAPIST: This?

* Philip Rieff, *Freud: The Mind of the Moralist* (New York: Doubleday, 1961); *Triumph of the Therapeutic* (New York: Harper, 1968); *Fellow Teachers* (New York: Dell, 1975). Ernest Becker, *The Denial of Death* (New York: Free Press, 1973).

CLIENT: Living, I mean.

THERAPIST: When did these thoughts start happening?

CLIENT: I've thought about it, off and on, in different ways, all my life. But they really got to me about six months ago. That's when my mother died.

THERAPST: Your mother's death really upset you?

CLIENT: Sure. I suddenly realized that all my work and plans could and would end, just like hers did. What I really want to know, to understand, is *what is my life all about?*

Answer 1: *Can we talk a little more about your mother?*

In this response, the therapist is exploring the possible connection between the client's intensity of feeling toward his mother and his experienced depression. Implicit in this question is the assumption that the client's concerns about his mortality, his dissatisfaction with work, and his questions about life's meaning are related to aspects of his psychological history. It follows from this view that if the client can confront and resolve his feelings toward his mother, and other psychological factors yet to be discovered, his depression and other concerns will be alleviated. He will no longer need to raise his question, since it will have found its own answer through the clarification and resolution of its underlying psychological causes.

In one sense, the therapist has not directly answered the client's question about the meaning of life. He has only raised another issue, which seems to have no relation to the original question. Yet, the therapist has tacitly answered the question by suggesting that the client's concern about life's meaning is symptomatic of unresolved psychological problems.

Answer 2: *If it helps, you're not alone in your concerns. What you're experiencing is what psychologists call midlife crisis. Often it is triggered by the loss of a parent. Let me assure you that people do come out on the other side of it.*

Here the therapist offers the reassurance that the client's problems are not unique and the comfort of knowing that there can be a positive outcome at the end of the crisis. It is not clear from the therapist's answer, nor is it evident from the adult development literature, whether the crisis must be allowed to run its course, or whether therapeutic intervention will be able to modify its extent and direction.

What is being communicated by this answer is that the client's depression and concerns about work, death, and life's meanings are somehow related to a commonly shared problem called midlife crisis. The fact that midlife crisis is a known and scientifically defined cause (or, seemingly, an underlying entity) of the client's problems indicates that his concerns are explainable, and perhaps capable of being controlled and modified.

Here again the client's question is not answered directly. The therapist's response rather refers the question to a state of affairs (midlife crisis) that is internal to the client's psychological world. Knowing that it is a shared concern lends it additional legitimacy, but it is still the individual's problem, not one that exists outside his psyche. What is being tacitly communicated is that the causes for raising the question are legitimate, explainable, and resolvable by dealing with the client's internal psychic life. There is no hint, however, as to the content of the resolution, of what actually is the meaning of the client's life.

What both these answers have in common is an implicit invalidation of the client's question. In pursuing the line of reasoning implied by each answer, the therapist is transforming the client's stated concerns into a form that the therapist (but not necessarily the client) feels is more appropriate and productive of solution. The client's problems and questions are now interpreted as being symptomatic of some aspect of his psychological make-up, whether acquired in his past history or through a midlife crisis.

But the client's concerns do have reference to a world outside his perceptions (or distortions, as the therapist might view them). Admittedly, what the world outside ourselves looks like is dependent upon us as perceivers. But this is self-evident. It becomes a hollow argument when it denies any validity or claim to truth of how the world actually is, independent of an individual's filtering. The client's dissatisfactions with work, for example, while understandable in terms of his perceptions of that world, must have some referent outside his perceptions. Something in the external world of work must have triggered his experienced dissatisfactions. And these work conditions were not created by his psyche. Similarly, his concern about the impact of death admittedly resides in his way of looking at it. But death and its effects on an individual's life plans and directions are independent of his psychological make-up. Further, to question life's meaning is not necessarily, as the therapist implicitly views it, a symptom of underlying psychological distress. The client's intent may be to obtain information and advice. His question could be understood as having similar intentions as in asking "What time of day is it?" or "Do you enjoy your job?" or "Where is the best place to buy a car?" The client's question is more than psychologically rhetorical if he is asking about a reality outside himself. This possibility is not thoroughly entertained in either of the previous two responses.

There is an important parallel to note in this collapsing of concerns about the external world into the client's individual psyche. The radical career changer has leveled many charges against the character of contemporary life. He maintains, among many claims, that the work life of a professional is most often repressive, without autonomy or real responsibility; that unnecessary, culturally created consumerism is antithetical to basic human values and needs; that the physical and psychological environment in which we live is fundamentally hostile and uninhabitable in terms of safety, interpersonal relationships, pace, and ecology. These statements could be seen, particularly from the psychological interpretive frame, as outgrowths of his personal psychological history or his shared midlife crisis. Thus these claims become suspect, viewed as only symptomatic of his underlying problem and distress.

And the psychological argument is, in one sense, true, except with a significant twist: had it not been for the radical career changer's distress, he may not have seen, with the clarity he did, what other people refuse to confront. What I am suggesting is a reversal of the therapeutic view. The distress, rather than necessarily leading to a distortion of the external world, may produce a fresh, critical look, a clarity of perception that most people do not or refuse to have. For example, Greg recognized the immorality implicit in the corporate coding, yet those who created it and those who worked within it failed to perceive it. Mark and Ron recognized that their clients were using human services not as a way of growing but as a sham for an unwillingness to change or for leading an immoral life. Are these perceptions simply the individual's personal distortions or do they make a real claim about what the world is like?

In the psychological interpretive frame, the external dimension is muted and the internal elevated; declarative statements tend to be viewed as distortions, without real meaning. In a very real sense, the radical career changer's claims were accorded more legitimacy by his nonsupportive friends back home than they would be given by the psychological frame. They did not invalidate the statements, as a therapist might, by flipping them back into the radical career changer's psychological world, thus blurring or obliterating the question of truth. Rather they accepted the statements as assertions about the world, as having a meaningful content that could be judged as true or false.

Why does the therapist tend to interpret claims and questions that may well be about the external world as products of internal psychological states? The answer to this question becomes more evident in examining the next response that the therapist could give to the client's question.

Answer 3: *The answer to your question lies in finding something to believe deeply in, to be totally committed to. This will provide you with a meaning to your life.*

This response is so incongruous, so far from what most people expect from a therapist, that it underlines the limits of the psychological frame. Although this answer is the only one that accepts the client's question as a request for information and advice, few therapists would answer in this way. Had he given that answer, the therapist would likely see himself and be perceived by others as being presumptuous; what gives him the right to tell people what to do with their lives?

And any possible presumption he might have would be checked by his role definition as a therapist, as a representative of the psychological interpretive frame. Historically, psychoanalysis (and subsequent psychotherapies) attempted to purge the individual's psychological world of the debilitating consequences of belief systems, ideologies, and culture. By helping a distressed person to understand and resolve how his early socialization, as an embodiment of his culture's prescriptions, affected his perceptions and behavior, the psychological frame freed him from unnecessary guilt and anxiety. Thus, as Freud dramatically demonstrated, Victorian repressive attitudes toward sexuality led to many maladaptive psychological responses that unduly reduced the individual's freedom of choice and happiness. The psychological frame of interpretation was able to remove the embodied cultural obstacles.

Although it has been one of the most significant advances in making our lives agreeable, this way of interpreting the world is, in the final analysis, destructive of belief. It throws into question the validity of all beliefs by demonstrating that they are accepted because of the individual's psychological needs and socialization. Such a collapsing of belief into the individual's psyche undermines any real claim that the belief makes about the external world. No one belief can be truer than another. All have similar underlying dynamics. All are equally suspect. Yet, the psychological frame provides no alternative answers.

The individual nevertheless needs beliefs. They provide necessary points of reference, the set of definitions from which he can meaningfully interpret his experience. Where is he to find them? He often tries in therapy (and sometimes in his reading of the popular literature) to elevate the therapist (or author) to the role of supreme authority and definer of boundaries (an action technically known as transference). But the therapist cannot allow himself to be made into a permanent guru. He cannot, by definition, provide answers to questions of meaning. If he does, then he must suspect himself, since belief in him is no different from other beliefs. Such belief arises out of psychological need. It is therefore suspect and ultimately destructive of unencumbered choice. Nor can the therapist as an individual, as a representative only of himself, necessarily provide better answers than his clients. He himself is likely to have similar concerns and unanswered questions about the meaning of life.

An individual has a great deal to gain from his encounter with a therapist. He can find support in knowing his concerns are shared and explainable; he can perhaps find needed relief from distress. But he cannot gain answers to his questions about the world outside, the meanings it has or could contain. He is thus thrown back upon himself to find those answers, a source that he originally found empty and without solutions. That is why, in part, he sought help and advice in therapy.

His question of life's meaning, moreover, belies the difficulty in the culture and, as represented in the therapist, of providing an acceptable frame of reference to define what are significant values and meanings in living. In the therapeutic world and society outside, these are either ignored, difficult to perceive, illusory, or questionable.

This lack, or denial, of external cultural definitions is also obvious in the stories of radical career changers. Mike, for example, believes only in himself and his family's needs. He believes, moreover, that all beliefs are dangerous and empty. He purposely isolates himself and his family from society. Society is an immoral antagonist, to be dealt with, if necessary, but never to be helped by his activities and commitments. His life seems aimless, shifting, structured only by the unseen, amorphous operation of "process." Like Mike, practically all the radical career changers believe primarily in themselves and their families. Self is paramount. The radical career changers actively seek it in the Santa Fe landscape—to be independent, to be themselves. This is the promise of Santa Fe. Even Greg's higher morality is primarily self-defined and personal. He is like Don Quixote except that he lacks the illusion of chivalric mission. And Ron, the former minister, believes more in himself and his personal search for God than in the religious system that originally defined his life. This personal embeddedness leads him to see only himself in the Truchas landscape.

The only exception to this world of personal definition is Steven. He is committed to the grander cause of creating an ecologically sensible world. His vision outside himself provides him with a mission, a fixity of purpose that makes intelligible his many shifts of environment and work. Everything is interpreted and made meaningful in terms of this overarching purpose. His goal is to make a positive contribution to society, to a social system and a myriad of institutions that he sees as misguided but capable of productive change through his efforts. His conflict arose out of the costly price exacted by his mission: it required him to sacrifice himself.

The significance of having a frame external to oneself was underlined for me by a sixty-eight-year-old friend. After reading a summary of my research, he commented: "I found what you were describing foreign to me. I've never had a midlife crisis—who could afford it? And a radical career change? Oh, I've heard of people doing it, but I don't have that choice, nor do I want it. You see, when I came over from Europe, that was in 1925, I needed to make a living. So I learned what was easy to pick up and paid the best salary. I became a counter-man in a delicatessen. I hated the work then, and I still hate it now. But who expected work to be meaningful and fulfilling? Work is work. That's all it is. It has to be done.

"I work because I need money to live. But surviving is not enough to justify slicing corned beef ten hours a day, six days a week. I can go in every day because I want my children to have more out of their lives than I did. Having more, not so much in terms of property or possessions, but more in terms of being able to choose a more meaningful life. I work for that and also for another reason—maybe the more important reason. I work for my day off, those happy Sundays where I can read and learn and study. That's when I feel alive. I study what other people have thought so I can think about important things. Dreaming, thinking, wondering—that's the life of the mind. That's what it means to be human, to get outside yourself, and understand how you and everything else fit together. There are just not enough Sundays in a life."

His tone was of gentle acceptance. The weight of responsibility is as heavy for him as for the radical career changer and the earlier-quoted middle-aged questioner. Yet he shoulders it with a quality of lightness, as a basis for satisfaction, without the burden of obligation. What has relieved some of the load is having a point of reference, a set of meanings, that acts as a leverage on living. Those happy Sundays provide him with a perspective that defines and makes intelligible his work and responsibility. They offer an illumination outside himself. By studying and incorporating the writings of other people, he can order his choices and activities. His needs and concerns take on the scale of being a part of a larger, broader set of meanings.

His Sundays are not simply escapes from the reality of the prior week, but represent a culmination, a meaningful capping, of all that has happened before. From the perspective of

Sunday, work assumes the role of a necessity for survival, an acceptable minor position in living. It allows for the life of the mind. He is not defined by his work, but rather defines himself and his life in terms of the outcomes of his Sundays. The seeming meaninglessness of work is not frustrating. It need not be meaningful since the important definitions occur on that capping day.

His choices are defined not only in terms of what is feasible but what is worth choosing. He is, in principle, as much a free agent as Max claimed to be. If he wanted, he could give up his work and responsibilities and go to Santa Fe. But he has no need to exercise that choice, which allowed Max and the others to be indepedent and to find themselves. He is already himself; his Sundays allow him to know who he is. That perspective shows him that he can maintain a sense of self during the rest of the week, in a work setting that, in any objective terms, is far more constrictive than any that the radical career changers had experienced. He is willing to accept the narrow limits of choice in his life because he does not perceive them as restrictions. They are just boundaries, relatively insignificant ones, as Sundays define them. He has found satisfaction and meaning within their confines. Thus, midlife crisis is unreal to him because its bases—of reaching previously established goals, dissatisfaction with work, renegotiated family needs, or the death of a parent—are all issues that form a part of the meanings defined by his frame of reference. They are not the frustrations of living but part of what defines a life.

His life of the mind is only one among many external frames that have been used to order and make sense out of existence. The radical career changer tried a different one: the cultural frame that work is a mission capable of defining a meaningful life. He found it empty of valid meaning. Moreover, the culture and the institutions that project this view are immoral in not sustaining that mission. In rejecting this external frame, the radical career changer could have selected among other available ones. In Santa Fe, for example, he could have chosen either of two dramatically clear sets of definitions: the Catholicism and family orientation of the Spanish culture or the strong traditions of the Indian world. He chose to adopt neither, not simply because he was partially excluded from participating in them, but, more significantly, because he was already embedded in another frame of reference upon arrival. Having experienced the death of his former externally defined meanings, and in choosing to leave "back home," he moved his frame inward, into himself. Here was a source of meaning and definition that he believed to be unassailable, that seemed to be absolutely valid.

Did this shift from the external to an internal frame work? Or, to put the question in the terms of my middle-aged questioner, "Is he happy?" Most radical career changers are, if "happy" means not having to deal with the frustrations of "back home." If "happy" is understood in more absolute terms, in relation to the actualities of their present lives, then they are sometimes happy, sometimes unhappy. Some are happier than others. There was no miraculous transformation into a beatific state of satisfaction that occurred with the move to Santa Fe. The contingencies of living—friendships, work, mortality—are the same everywhere.

Perhaps happiness is not the appropriate criterion. It is a measure that already assumes a self-oriented internal frame of reference. Without the anchoring of some external point, the definition of what constitutes being happy becomes relative, individual, and nonspecific in time. A suggestive point in this regard was made by George Vaillant in his study of adult development in a group of Harvard graduates: "I was 33, they were 46. . . . I was alarmed by what I had learned about the next decade of life, and I rushed to discuss my experience with my 54-year-old department chairman. 'I don't want to grow up,' I explained to my chief. 'These men are all so . . . so depressed.' As I was to learn, the men were by no means despairing; but, like any child first discovering the facts of life,

I had suddenly distorted what I had seen. In part . . . the men had grown up enough to acknowledge the real pain that I, who had not reached their stage of life, still denied." *

What the question "Are they happy?" is asking for, on another level, is a guarantee that the radical solution does work. The middle-aged man who raised this question, I, and the many other people who are seeking this assurance share the awareness that our external frames, particularly that work is a defining force of life, do not function well. We are caught in the web of former meanings that have turned oppressive. In our search for a way out, a guarantee of success would make the solution of going far away, to the Santa Fe's out there, a more palatable option. Unfortunately, the guarantee is ambiguous: it has no clear measure of success nor any consistency of outcome.

Yet the decision to change radically or not may be less problematic than it appears on the surface. In terms of available reference frames, the distance between Santa Fe and "back home" may be closer than the dramatic change in work, income, status, and living landscape that such a move would suggest. What originally seemed to be a polarized choice without any intermediate solution may be little choice at all. In relation to the cultural embeddedness in which these choices occur, the Santa Fe's out there and "back home" are fundamentally similar places. They share in the same internal frame of reference of the self where the external frames available have been rejected as having little meaning or value in interpreting experience.

There are many valid reasons for the rejection of such available external frames as political ideology, religion, family, or work. Blind, uncritical affiliation with political systems has led to massive destruction. Cultural frames, embodied in childhood socialization, have limited personal freedom and choice. The discrepancies between the ideals projected by external frames and the actualities of their operation maintain

---

* *Adaptation to Life* (Boston: Little, Brown, 1977), p. 195.

disillusionment. How can an individual believe in work as a social mission when his efforts are obliterated in an endless chain of bureaucracy whose primary goal is its own self-preservation? How long can a person believe in the democratic ideal of freedom and equality for all when some are treated as more equal than others?

This chronicling of the bases for rejecting external frames could be extended endlessly. What is important to understand is that all these reasons, whether taken singly or in combination, have led many people to believe that any commitment to an external frame can lead to little else except the destructive faith of a Manson family or the seemingly mindless chanting of the Krishna sect. The toll of this legitimate cynicism is to leave the individual and the culture without any viable frame of reference except the internal reference of self.

The orientation toward self has been sustained, and in part created, by the human sciences (for example, psychology, anthropology, sociology). The continuous proliferation of psychological aids—self-help books and a never-ending array of therapies—has become a commonplace in contemporary American culture. These sources of knowledge and help for the self have increasingly been elevated by their consumers to the status of an external frame, a place that cannot be readily justified. Therapists now become gurus, self-help books projecting self-actualization, "doing your thing" or knowing yourself become Bible-like sources for finding the happy, satisfying life. Gail Sheehy's best-selling book, *Passages*, which popularizes the adult development literature, has been raised, by many adults, to such an esteemed status. Her ideals of growth and self-fulfillment as goals in living are accepted uncritically because they appear to be part of the scientific study of adult development. Yet the book never justifies whether such growth has any purpose and direction other than growing or personal satisfaction. This omission is not simply an oversight but rather an indicator that the book's internal frame can be supported only by an appeal to itself.

Such elevation of the human sciences is just one of the

myriad examples of the pervasive need of individuals to have some external frame of reference. Ernest Becker says it seems that "modern man cannot find his heroism in everyday life any more, as men did in traditional societies just by doing their daily duty of raising children, working, and worshipping. He needs revolutions and wars and 'continuing' revolutions to last when the revolutions and wars end. That is the price modern man pays for the eclipse of the sacred dimension. When he dethroned the ideas of soul and God he was thrown back hopelessly on his own resources, on himself and those few around him. Even lovers and families trap and disillusion us because they are not substitutes for absolute transcendence." * For all the destructive possibilities of external frames, the individual needs something outside himself to define who he is. A self only for itself has little dimension. As the theologian Hillel put the issue nearly two thousand years ago: "If I am not for myself, who is for me? And if I am only for myself, what am I?"

Nor can a society or a culture maintain itself when its members live primarily for themselves and share only marginally in its public life. While the culture has the responsibility of providing viable external frames, its subscribers must reciprocate by their responsible involvement in their maintenance and evolution.

A culture's external frames must fall of their own weight if its member's primary commitment is to self. A society cannot continue when its participants forgo contributing their talents to the common good for the sake of personal satisfaction. Marginal groups who choose to dismiss their societal commitments, whether bohemians, beats, hippies, or contemporary radical career changers, can be tolerated only when they are the exception to the rule of public commitment of talent and ability. Beyond that limit, a culture or a society ceases to be communal and actual. It becomes a hollow structure incapable

* *The Denial of Death* (New York: Free Press, 1973), p. 190.

of binding its members together. All that remains is a world of individual, unrelated, separate selves.*

In these terms, the answer to the radical career changers' search for meaning and that of many others who share their concerns is simply to find a viable external frame of reference to define meaning and purpose. This answer seems so self-evident and obvious, yet it is difficult to accept. Our contemporary disillusionment with any external frames blinds us to seeing this answer and makes us distrust its presence.

But saying that an external perspective is necessary for a meaningful life is far too easy an answer; moreover, it is not a convincing one. The more significant and compelling question is "What is that frame to be?" Can there be a meaningful external perspective that can define meaning yet does not endanger personal freedom and life? The real challenge offered by the lives of the radical career changers is for individuals and society to innovate new external frames that can effectively overcome our justified suspicion of all frames.

An important first step in meeting this challenge is to clarify the issues involved in a frame's construction and acceptance. A partial source of such illumination may be found in the human sciences, of which the adult development literature forms a part.

The human sciences have evolved as distinct, generally non-overlapping fields of study. Each has its specific focus and competence. Psychology has made its concern the life of the individual, while the study of his cultural embeddedness is left primarily to anthropology. The anthropologist, in turn, does an acceptable job in providing a differentiated analysis of culture but leaves the individual encapsulated, almost as a nondescript pawn being moved within a rich cultural texture. The psychologist and the anthropologist then leave to the historian the analysis of how the individual and his culture

---

* See Richard Sennett, *The Fall of Public Man* (New York: Knopf, 1977), for an analysis of this complex of issues.

stand in relation to the past. What emerges from this disciplinary separateness is a series of narrowly focused fields, each doing a reasonable job in its domain. The more meaningful, comprehensive picture is bequeathed to the unfilled interstices between them.*

Such professional narrowness produces serious distortions in understanding complex social issues. The emerging adult development literature and its analysis of midlife crisis provides a good case in point. There is no question that individuals do experience this state of distress. Nor is there any question that psychologists and psychiatrists are capable of analyzing its determinants and its development. The emphasis of the research has been, and likely will continue to be, on the individual's responses to changing life situations and increasing age. What is not fully accepted or considered is that the midlife transition is inextricably tied to a particular state of our culture at a particular historical juncture. By not recognizing these historical and cultural factors, the adult development literature severely limits its generalizability and significance.

For example, most of the people interviewed in these studies were generally successful, upper-middle-class, predominantly male white-collar workers or professionals. These individuals are most likely to experience the greatest discrepancy between cultural projections and the actuality of knowing that these projections are partially illusory. They are also in the financial and status positions to believe that they have a large range of choice. Yet they often find that for all the abundance of options, the choices too often resemble each other. While these experiences are admittedly personal and intrapsychic, they are in part produced in interaction with the external agents of a culture and its social institutions.

---

* The range of issues and problems produced by the present disciplinary ethnocentricism is admirably analyzed by Donald Campbell in "Ethnocentricism of Disciplines and the Fish Scale Model of Omniscience," in Muzafer Sherif and Carolyn W. Sherif (eds.), *Interdisciplinary Relationships in the Social Sciences* (Chicago: Aldine, 1969).

Moreover, these personal-cultural interactions must be placed in historical perspective. Viewed thus, many people in midlife crisis today seem to live in a world of collapsing external frames, a pattern that has been slowly and imperceptibly evolving. The evolution of such changes can be seen even in the present moment. In the life of a forty-year-old person, there are likely to be people who represent different stages in the progression of shifting frames: his parents likely believe in a more external frame and societal mission; he is likely to be ambivalent as to whether there can be any meaningful external perspective; his children are likely to have moved to the other side of disillusionment into a more internally focused orientation.

By incorporating these historical and cultural factors, the personal phenomenon of midlife crisis now takes on the character of being more a disorder of interpretive frames that promise but do not fulfill expectation than solely a problem of the individual's internal developmental life. If the focus is placed primarily on the individual, as in the adult development literature, then the implied action in remedying or relieving the distress becomes misplaced. The literature's tendency to focus on the internal life, and with it the collapsing of his concerns about the external world into the psyche, avoids the necessary analysis of the interaction between the individual's developmental changes and the external conditions that define and often create the difficulty. Rather than raise the question "What is it about our culture and our time that makes the death of a parent the basis for questioning a life?" the literature simply suggests that there is a link between these two events. Rather than ask "What is it about our culture and our time that inappropriately elevates work to a mission?" the literature points to the frustration of that mission as one basis for midlife crisis.

The studies of adult development are good as far as they go. But they do not go far enough. And this emptiness, on the other side of empirical fact, is where the danger lies. People could easily come to mistake what is described as possible, as all that there is. The literature creates the unreal expectation that by modifying the way the individual perceives his world his difficulties in living in that world will be overcome. Neither the literature's implied internalistic frame nor its suggested acceptance and accommodation to the culture and its institutions is likely to fully and effectively resolve the issues involved in midlife crisis. The pressures of the world will not disappear by treating the person's psyche. Researchers have begun to understand this point in helping the mentally disturbed. They know that a person, having been helped to well-being in the isolation of a mental hospital, can readily break down again under the stress of the environment to which he ultimately returns. Yet the investigators in the area of adult development do not recognize the parallel for the person in midlife transition. Unless the stress produced by the individual's social embeddedness is modified, his midlife crisis will continue and become a shared commonplace in our culture. The literature's implicit philosophy of personal accommodation to what are often immoral and destructive external situations undermines the possibility of a meaningful life.

But a deeper level of analysis than this is required if the changing life of an adult is to be put in its appropriate perspective. What is needed is a study of the broad questions about individuals' affiliation with frames of reference. With the exception of the Freudian literature on transference,* there is very little available in human sciences research to answer these questions. Under what conditions does an individual affiliate with a frame of reference? How can one differentiate between an uncritical and a critical acceptance of a frame of reference? What criteria can be used to understand and predict whether a frame of reference will be valuable for an individual and/or a culture? In what relation does an internal frame stand to an

---

* See Becker, *The Denial of Death*, chapter 7, for an excellent critical analysis of this literature.

external frame in providing intelligibility to an individual's life?

These questions have no ready answers. Nor are they answerable by any one of the present human sciences. Their illumination requires the integration of all these disciplines' concerns, so that the individual can be meaningfully understood in all his relevant contexts. Only with such understanding can we, as individuals and members of a culture, begin to accept the challenges posed by the lives of the radical career changers.

Because of these challenges I have written this book. The lives of the radical career changers I interviewed are fascinating as human interest items but uninstructive if they add just another set of data to the narrowly focused adult development literature. Their lives take on significance in the larger context of what those lives imply. In terms of our present cultural situation, their experiences and concerns raise the difficult question as to how we are to define our work and our lives. The crises in their life situations forced them to examine themselves from a critical distance, a vantage point from which at least their cultural embeddedness became clearer. Their stories, in turn, can provide us with a similar perspective. To pass off the radical career changers as people with "personal problems" is to avoid the issues they raise. We all share their problems. The seeds of radical career change and Santa Fe are within all of us.